Front endsheet: John F. Kennedy during the 1960 campaign; Bruce Roberts from Rapho-Guillumette. Back endsheet: Korean welcome for President and Mrs. Johnson; U.S. Army. Front cover: John F. Kennedy, Wide World; walk in space, Wide World; Lyndon Johnson in Australia, U.S. Army. Back cover: Jacqueline Kennedy, Wide World; helicopter in Vietnam, Wide World; J. F. K. button, Stanley King Collection; Dr. Martin Luther King, Jr., Wide World; Johnson addressing Congress, Wide World.

VOLUME

12

THE
AMERICAN HERITAGE
BOOK OF THE
PRESIDENTS
AND FAMOUS AMERICANS

★ ★ ★ ★ ★

JOHN FITZGERALD KENNEDY
LYNDON BAINES JOHNSON

CREATED AND DESIGNED BY THE EDITORS OF
AMERICAN HERITAGE
The Magazine of History

12-VOLUME EDITION PUBLISHED BY
DELL PUBLISHING CO., INC., NEW YORK, N.Y.

John Fitzgerald Kennedy

Lyndon Baines Johnson

CONTENTS
OF VOLUME TWELVE

FAMOUS AMERICANS

THE THIRTY-FIFTH PRESIDENT (1961–1963)

JOHN FITZGERALD KENNEDY

Just after sunset on the evening of August 1, 1943, fifteen PT boats moved out of Rendova Harbor in the South Pacific's Solomon Islands. Word had come that the Japanese would be moving in large force that night toward neighboring Kolombangara Island, and every available American boat had been ordered out into Blackett Strait on patrol duty.

To the men on board the departing PT boats, the Southern Cross was briefly visible amidst the early evening stars. Then the cloud bank that had been wrapped around Rendova Peak spread into a dark overcast and drifted out over Ferguson Passage, the waterway leading to Blackett Strait. The hours of patrol passed slowly, and on one of the PT boats a seaman was asking his skipper about his personal recollections of Winston Churchill. The boat's commander, twenty-six-year-old Lieutenant (junior grade) John Fitzgerald Kennedy, could easily oblige the man's curiosity, for he was the son of a former American ambassador to Great Britain's Court of St. James's and had moved easily in international diplomatic and political circles.

A 1940 graduate of Harvard University, Kennedy had been named an ensign in the United States Naval Reserve in October, 1941, and had been ordered to duty in the Pentagon. When Japan attacked Pearl Harbor on December 7, he had immediately requested sea duty. Not until the following year, however, was he sent to the PT boat-training school that led to his South Pacific assignment in April, 1943.

Not long after midnight, on August 2, Lieutenant Kennedy maneuvered *PT-109* near two other boats and suggested that they reverse their direction and make another sweep of Blackett Strait. There was no sign of the enemy in the inky blackness. Some minutes later, a man on board Kennedy's boat sud-

John F. Kennedy

denly shouted, "Ship at two o'clock!" The young officer had only a moment to glance up at the huge, looming prow cutting through a phosphorescent wave. In less than a minute it had sliced through *PT-109*. The stern, just behind Kennedy, went down in an instant, carrying two of the thirteen men on board to their death. Gasoline tanks burst into fire, and the survivors struggled against the suction of the passing ship only to surface into curtains of flame.

The Japanese destroyer *Amagiri* disappeared into the night. The other PT boats, having failed in attempts to destroy the enemy ship, raced for their home base. Kennedy had been hurled backward against the rear wall of the cockpit by the impact of the collision. Ensign George "Barney" Ross, a friend of Kennedy's who had merely come along for the ride that night, awoke from a faint to find himself in the water. In the engine room, Patrick McMahon—at thirty-seven the "old man" of *PT-109*—had been severely burned. The other eight men seemed not to have been seriously injured.

In the blackness of the night, Kennedy helped round up the survivors until all were either on or clinging to the floating hulk of *PT-109*'s forward section. Through the early morning hours of Monday, August 2, the men idly discussed whether they would fight or surrender if the Japanese appeared. When the hulk gave signs of sinking, Kennedy ordered his men to swim to a nearby island. Holding on to a plank so they would not become separated, nine of the men began kicking off toward shore. McMahon was too badly burned to swim, and so Kennedy clamped his teeth on the man's life preserver strap and set out to tow him to shore. It took them four hours to swim to a tiny islet.

That night Kennedy walked out on a coral reef as far as he could go and then swam to the middle of Ferguson Passage, where he waited for several hours in the forlorn hope that another PT boat patrol would spot him. The following night Barney Ross made a similar attempt to get help, but those two nights the PT boats were on a sweep elsewhere. On Wednesday, August 4, Kennedy

moved his pathetic party some two miles across an inlet to a larger island, where they hoped to find food. Again Kennedy used his teeth to tow McMahon.

Still desperate for food, Kennedy and Ross swam to a third island on Thursday. They found a wrecked Japanese vessel with a case of hard candy, which Kennedy took back to the second island. His men, the surprised lieutenant discovered, had visitors—natives working for the Allied forces. Carrying a message scratched on a coconut shell, the natives informed Allied agents in the area of the survivors. Other natives took Kennedy to the island of Gomu, and soon his party was rescued.

A brief eighteen years later, the hero of *PT-109* would stand on a platform outside the Capitol in Washington and on a bitterly cold but brilliantly clear January day proclaim: "Let the word go forth from this time and place, to friend and foe alike, that the torch has been passed to a new generation of Americans—born in this century, tempered by war, disciplined by a hard and bitter peace, proud of our ancient heritage. . . ."

The thirty-fifth President was born into an aristocracy—that of the Boston Irish. The 1914 marriage of his parents, Joseph Patrick Kennedy and Rose Fitzgerald, had been solemnized by William Cardinal O'Connell, for it united two of the city's most politically prominent families. Rose's father, the affable John F. "Honey Fitz" Fitzgerald, had been mayor of Boston. Joseph's father, Patrick J. Kennedy, was a former state representative and one of Boston's most powerful ward bosses.

Joseph P. Kennedy bypassed politics as a means of gaining power and took a more direct route—high finance. When he had been out of Harvard University for less than two years, he borrowed enough money to win control of a small East Boston bank; at twenty-five he was hailed as the nation's youngest bank president. The home in which Rose and Joseph P. Kennedy started their marriage was a gray frame dwelling in middle-class Brookline, Massachusetts. It was in this house that their first two sons were born:

Joseph P., Jr., in 1915, and, on May 29, 1917, John Fitzgerald Kennedy.

During World War I Joseph Kennedy served as assistant general manager of Bethlehem Steel Company's Quincy, Massachusetts, shipyard, where he had some rather strained dealings with the dynamic but highhanded assistant secretary of the Navy, Franklin D. Roosevelt. When the war ended, Kennedy entered the investment house of Hayden, Stone and Company and started to build his first million. By the end of the 1920's, the shrewd and ambitious young Irish-American had made his mark in securities, real estate, and the new movie industry. In 1925 he established the first of three trust funds that would make each of his children a multimillionaire.

The following year Joseph Kennedy moved his business operations—and his growing family—to New York. But after 1928 a rambling summer house at Hyannis Port on Massachusetts' Cape Cod was the clan's real home. By that time, in addition to Joseph, Jr., and John, there were Rosemary, Kathleen, Eunice, Patricia, Robert, and Jean. With eight children, the proud parents named a sailboat they had acquired the *Tenovus.* The arrival of their ninth and last child, Edward ("Teddy"), in February, 1932, coincided with the purchase of a new boat, appropriately called *Onemore.*

In later years much would be made of the influence John F. Kennedy's father and older brother had exerted on him. A certain amount of the father's often ruthless drive was transmitted to the entire family. Even in family sports, such as swimming, sailboat racing, and touch football games on the lawn at Hyannis Port, each Kennedy was taught to play to win.

In his early years, John Kennedy too often found himself in the shadow of Joe, Jr. At Choate, an exclusive preparatory school in Wallingford, Connecticut, Joe won the Harvard Trophy for his combined success in sports and scholarship. Young Jack, a "gentleman C scholar," finished sixty-fourth in a class of one hundred and twelve. Partly to avoid further competition with his brother, Jack decided not to follow Joe to Harvard, but enrolled instead at Princeton. However, during a summer visit to England, where he studied briefly at the London School of Eco-

The picture above shows Lieutenant (j.g.) John F. Kennedy arriving at Gomu Island in the Solomons after his rescue by natives during World War II. Kennedy and his PT boat crew had been marooned on another island.

Ambassador to Great Britain Joseph P. Kennedy took his two oldest sons to England in 1938. John, left, and Joseph, Jr., right, who had engaged in fierce fist fights as children, had become friendly rivals.

nomics, he contracted jaundice. His illness forced Jack to start late at Princeton, and a recurrence of the ailment caused him to drop out of college during the Christmas recess. In the fall of 1936 he entered Harvard. In his first two years he was again a C student.

Meanwhile, Joseph P. Kennedy had seen his old adversary from the Quincy shipyard days, Franklin D. Roosevelt, elected President in 1932. Two years later Kennedy was appointed to the Securities and Exchange Commission, one of Roosevelt's New Deal reforms, and served as its first chairman, from July, 1934, to September, 1935. During the 1936 presidential campaign Joseph Kennedy published a book, *I'm for Roosevelt*, which endeared him to F. D. R. His reward for this campaign support was appointment, in December, 1937, as ambassador to the Court of St. James's.

His father's new position gave Jack access to many of Europe's most influential men. Taking off the second semester of his junior year at Harvard, he traveled across Europe, including Russia, as the storm clouds of World War II were gathering. Back in London on September 1, 1939, when Hitler's invasion of Poland finally triggered the war in Europe, Jack Kennedy caught his first

glimpse of conflict when he went to Scotland to help American survivors of a torpedoed British ship, the *Athenia*.

Sobered by his experiences in Europe, young Kennedy returned to Harvard and in his senior year became a candidate for a degree with honors in political science. His undergraduate thesis, a study of Allied appeasement of Hitler, was later published under the title *Why England Slept* and became a best seller.

During the winter of 1939–40 Joseph Kennedy grew increasingly pessimistic about Britain's chances of survival, and after the fall of France in June, 1940, he began to think of Hitler's triumph as inevitable. In December he resigned his ambassadorship to return to the United States to champion nonintervention. After Pearl Harbor, Kennedy volunteered for service with F. D. R.'s wartime administration but was never given another government assignment. Thus, as his oldest sons donned uniforms, his influence in government receded.

Four months after Lieutenant John F. Kennedy's dramatic rescue in the Solomon Islands, he was rotated back to the States. He had contracted malaria, and the fall he had taken at the time of the collision with the *Amagiri* had aggravated a back injury sustained a few years earlier during a football game at college. A disc operation was performed on his back at the Chelsea Naval Hospital near Boston. It was while he was a patient there that Jack learned that his older brother, Joe, Jr., had been killed during an air mission over Europe.

Early in 1945 Jack was separated from the service. Through his father, he got a job as a writer with Hearst's International News Service and covered the founding of the United Nations in San Francisco. A journalist's career was not likely to satisfy either Jack or his father, however. Kennedy had confided to a close friend, Paul B. "Red" Fay, that he would soon be "trying to parlay a lost PT boat and a bad back into a political advantage."

A persistent legend about the Kennedy family is that Joseph P. Kennedy had slated his eldest son for the White House and that when Joe, Jr., was killed, Jack was drafted for the job. Whatever the validity of such a tale, early in 1946 John F. Kennedy announced his candidacy for United States representative from Massachusetts' Eleventh Congressional District in East Boston.

After an absence of twenty years, the Kennedys returned to Boston—to campaign for Jack. Honey Fitz, a spry octogenarian, was dusted off to sing "Sweet Adeline" for sentimental old-timers, but in all other respects the campaign was a modern blitz. Old friends from Choate and Harvard were enlisted in the crusade, and Navy buddies flocked in from across the country to call attention to the candidate's war record. The attractive Kennedy ladies, mother and sisters, fanned out across the district to attend campaign tea parties and to hand out literature. Twenty-year-old brother Bobby, also just home from the Navy, took over the campaign in one particularly difficult area. There was a heavy advertising budget, and a reprint of a *Reader's Digest* article about *PT-109* was widely distributed.

Overcoming charges of carpetbagging and vote buying on his father's part, Jack Kennedy won the Democratic primary by a 2 to 1 plurality over his nearest opponent.

In East Boston, the Democratic nomination was as good as election, and he won easily in November. Two years later, in 1948, he had no Republican rival at all; and in 1950 he was elected to a third term in the House of Representatives by a ratio of 5 to 1.

Only twenty-nine years old when he first took his seat in Congress in January, 1947, Jack Kennedy was occasionally mistaken for an elevator operator. He was one of a minority opposing the conservative Taft-Hartley labor bill and he unsuccessfully supported federal aid to housing. In foreign affairs Congressman Kennedy was a maverick. He blamed President Truman and Secretary of State Marshall for the loss of China to the Communists in 1949 and criticized the administration's defense-spending policies. Yet he did not strongly endorse Truman's intervention in Korea and voted to trim economic aid abroad.

After his re-election in 1948 Kennedy began to think of higher office—either governor or United States senator from Massachusetts. He began spending four-day weekends in Massachusetts, ranging far from his district to make political speeches. In April, 1952, he announced that he would oppose the re-election of Senator Henry Cabot Lodge II. The contest, in a sense, was a rerun of the 1916 senatorial election in which Lodge's grandfather, Henry Cabot Lodge, Sr., had defeated Honey Fitz. But Jack was running as an entirely different kind of candidate from his grandfather. He was, said a fellow politician, "the first Irish Brahmin."

The familiar Kennedy barrage of billboards, tea parties, and reprints of the *Reader's Digest* article was loosed. And on Election Day in November, 1952, Kennedy defeated Lodge by more than 70,000 votes, while Eisenhower carried the state for the Republicans by more than 200,000 votes.

Two of the most notable accomplishments of his Senate years had nothing to do with politics. On September 12, 1953, he married the talented and beautiful Jacqueline Bouvier at a glittering Newport, Rhode Island, ceremony. And in 1955 Kennedy wrote *Profiles in Courage*, the best-selling book that would win him a Pulitzer Prize for biography. The writing of the book was the outgrowth of another major occurrence of his early senatorial years, one that nearly brought a tragic end to his career.

Through his years in Congress, Kennedy continued to be plagued with a bad back, and by the summer of 1954 he could get about only on crutches. Told that a spinal-fusion operation involved serious risk, he slapped his crutches and said bitterly: "I'd rather die than spend the rest of my life on these things." Twice following an operation that October, Kennedy was close to death, and he survived only to learn that the surgery had not been fully successful. A second operation was performed in February, 1955. Kennedy's

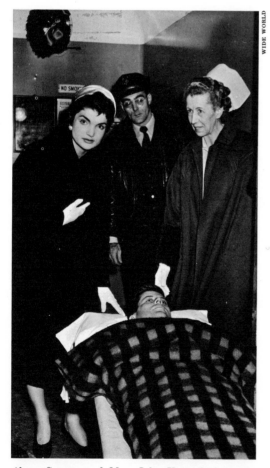

Above, Senator and Mrs. John Kennedy leave the hospital after his October, 1954, spinal operation. In February he returned for additional surgery.

back condition was never completely cured. At a 1961 tree-planting ceremony in Canada he once more injured his back, and thereafter he reportedly never had a day without pain.

Kennedy spent the early months of 1955 recuperating at his father's Palm Beach, Florida, home. He used this period of forced inactivity to research and write *Profiles in Courage*, biographical sketches of senators who had put principles ahead of politics.

During Kennedy's illness, in December, 1954, the Senate had voted to condemn Wisconsin's Senator Joseph McCarthy for his irresponsible crusade against Communists in government. Kennedy's failure to pair or to announce his position on this issue was later the basis for attacks on his own political courage. McCarthy, like Kennedy a Roman Catholic, had a large and vociferous following, including many Boston Irish, outside Wisconsin.

Friends later speculated that Kennedy's decision to seek the Presidency was made during his months of convalescence in Florida. The following year, 1956, was a presidential election year, but the unsuccessful Democratic standard-bearer of 1952, Adlai E. Stevenson, was clearly going to be given a second try at the office. Following his expected renomination, Stevenson dramatically left open to the convention the selection of a vice presidential candidate. As millions watched on television, Kennedy ran neck and neck with Senator Estes Kefauver of Tennessee for two ballots, only to lose to him on the third.

Jack Kennedy's tireless campaigning for the Stevenson-Kefauver ticket won the admiration of his fellow politicians. In 1958 he was re-elected to the Senate by a majority of 874,608 votes. Backed by this impressive endorsement, he became the favorite for the 1960 vice presidential nomination. "I'm not running for Vice-President any more," Kennedy told one Democrat, however. "I'm now running for President."

The Kennedy candidacy, according to Theodore H. White, was launched at a meeting held by sixteen people in Robert Ken-

While convalescing from his 1955 back operation, Jack Kennedy painted this Mediterranean scene.

nedy's house at Hyannis Port on October 28, 1959. The senator and his associates, who included his father and two brothers, were to make a President, White has written, "with greater precision, against greater odds, across more contrary traditions, than had been shown by any group of amateur President makers since Abraham Lincoln's backers, a century before, had changed the structure of nineteenth-century politics."

With the lamentable exception of Warren G. Harding, no man had gone directly from the United States Senate to the Presidency. Curiously, three of Kennedy's rivals for the 1960 Democratic nomination were fellow senators—Hubert H. Humphrey of Minnesota, Stuart Symington of Missouri, and Lyndon B. Johnson of Texas. In the background, waiting for the lightning strike of a third nomination, was Adlai E. Stevenson of Illinois.

To prove false the political axiom that no Roman Catholic could be elected President, Kennedy decided he would have to fight for the nomination in the primaries. When he announced his candidacy on January 2, 1960, he declared his intention of facing the electorate in the New Hampshire primary, the earliest in the nation, the following March. To no one's surprise he rolled up an impressive vote from his fellow New Englanders. The major tests, however, would be in Wis-

consin and West Virginia, in both of which he would be facing the redoubtable Hubert Humphrey. Symington and Stevenson remained inactive candidates, each hoping for a deadlocked convention. Lyndon Johnson said that he was too busy as Senate Majority Leader to campaign.

The blitz technique, developed in the earlier Kennedy campaigns in Massachusetts, was transferred full scale to Wisconsin in April, 1960. An important addition was the Kennedy family airplane, a converted Convair named for the senator's daughter, Caroline, born in 1957. Running against the Kennedys, Humphrey complained, was "like an independent retailer competing with a chain." (Kennedy brushed aside complaints that family money was buying the election by reading at a dinner in New York City an imaginary wire from his father: "Dear Jack: Don't buy one vote more than necessary. I'll be damned if I'll pay for a landslide.") On April 5 Kennedy captured 56 per cent of the vote in the Wisconsin primary. But the result was not decisive; he would have to meet Humphrey once again on May 10 in West Virginia.

Kennedy had selected the West Virginia battleground with care. The predominantly Protestant state—only 5 per cent of its population was Catholic—was also one of the poorest in the Union. If a Catholic and a rich man's son could win there, Kennedy reasoned, he could win anywhere. And so it proved. Jack Kennedy carried the primary with 61 per cent of the vote, and Humphrey was forced to withdraw as a candidate.

Led by Bobby Kennedy, the senator's campaign staff had been quietly and inexorably rounding up delegates in states without primaries. Before the July 11 opening of the convention in Los Angeles, Kennedy had 600 of the 761 votes needed to win the nomination. There was still opposition, however. In a withering attack, former President Harry S. Truman questioned the senator's maturity. If elected at the age of forty-three, Kennedy would be the second youngest man to serve in the White House. (Theodore Roosevelt, who became President when he was forty-two, was the youngest.) In a brilliant rebuttal, Kennedy pointed out that his fourteen years in Congress gave him more government experience than all but a few Presidents—not including Truman—had had at the time of their accession to the office. A further challenge was posed by the venerable Mrs. Eleanor Roosevelt, who urged Stevenson's renomination.

Despite these obstacles, Kennedy's nomination came, almost anticlimactically, on the first ballot. His closest rival, Lyndon B. Johnson, was promptly offered, and accepted, the vice presidential nomination. According to some reports, Kennedy had not really expected the proud and sensitive Johnson to take the second spot, but the choice of the Texan was a shrewd one. It healed party wounds and gave geographical and religious balance to the ticket.

In one of the early addresses of his campaign, Kennedy moved to eliminate his religion as a political issue. The platform he chose was a daring one, a meeting of the Greater Houston Ministerial Association in Texas. There, to a largely hostile audience, he pledged that his Catholicism would in no way hamper the exercise of his presidential duties. He believed, as firmly as they did, he said, in the separation of church and state.

Many political observers felt that the election was won by Kennedy in the series of four television debates held in September and October with his Republican opponent, Richard M. Nixon. Before audiences estimated at sixty-five to seventy million Americans, a relaxed and self-confident John F. Kennedy traded words with an often tired and uncertain Nixon.

On Election Day, November 8, 1960, John F. Kennedy was elected President by the narrowest popular margin in the twentieth century. Only 113,057 votes out of nearly 69,000,000 cast separated Kennedy and Nixon. "So now my wife and I prepare for a new administration, and a new baby," he said in acknowledging Nixon's concession. Sixteen days later, John, Jr., was born.

In accepting the Democratic nomination the preceding July, Kennedy had enunciated his doctrine of the New Frontier and had said that it "sums up not what I intend to *offer* the American people, but what I intend to *ask* of them." The New Frontier was defined as "uncharted areas of science and space, unsolved problems of peace and war, unconquered pockets of ignorance and prejudice, unanswered questions of poverty and surplus." The American people, Kennedy insisted, were at a turning point "between the public interest and private comfort, between national greatness and national decline, between the fresh air of progress and the stale, dank atmosphere of 'normalcy.' "

On January 20, 1961, John F. Kennedy; in one of history's most stirring Inaugural Addresses, pledged himself to get the country moving again. "Now the trumpet summons us again—not as a call to bear arms, though arms we need—not as a call to battle, though embattled we are—but a call to bear the burden of a long twilight struggle year in and year out, 'rejoicing in hope, patient in tribulation'—a struggle against the common enemies of man: tyranny, poverty, disease and war itself. . . . And so, my fellow Americans: ask not what your country can do for you—ask what you can do for your country."

As Kennedy announced his choices for the Cabinet and for an expanded White House staff, comparisons began to be made between F. D. R.'s New Deal Brain Trust and J. F. K.'s New Frontiersmen. Harvard and MIT, it was said, would soon lose all their professors to Washington.

Because of the Kennedy style and Kennedy wit his live press conferences were among television's most entertaining shows. On the New Frontier the men seemed more brilliant and efficient, the women more charming and attractive, the social gatherings gayer.

Along more serious lines, the Food for Peace program, initiated during Eisenhower's administration, was taken over by the Kennedy administration in an effort to solve the problem of agricultural surpluses at home while winning friends abroad. Borrowing an idea from Senators Hubert Humphrey and Richard Neuberger, the President announced on March 1, 1961, the formation of the Peace Corps, which would send volunteer workers to underdeveloped countries. At an impressive White House gathering of Latin-American diplomats on March 13, he launched the Alliance for Progress, an ambitious program for economic cooperation and social development.

Political commentators made new comparisons between F. D. R. and Kennedy, writing of a second Hundred Days that would duplicate or even surpass the accomplishments of Roosevelt's first three months in office. Then came the Bay of Pigs.

During the closing months of the Eisenhower administration, the Central Intelligence Agency had begun training a force of anti-Castro Cubans in a Guatemalan jungle camp. Between his election and inauguration, John F. Kennedy learned of the plans to land this force in Cuba in an attempt to overthrow the Cuban dictator, who had taken his island into the Communist camp. New to his office, Kennedy let the professional intelligence and military men talk him into endorsing the invasion. Early in April, the force was put ashore at Cuba's Bay of Pigs—and was easily repelled by Castro. The debacle cost Kennedy the support of liberals at home and resulted in a great loss of prestige abroad.

A second international crisis loomed in Southeast Asia, where the United States moved close to intervention in Laos but settled for an international conference that established a neutral country.

Curious to meet the adversary who could cause him so much trouble in far corners of the globe, Kennedy arranged a rendezvous in Vienna in June with Russia's Nikita Khrushchev. The two days of talks were grim and unproductive, serving only to demonstrate the resolution and inflexibility that separated East and West. Khrushchev threatened to isolate the Western enclave in Berlin by signing a separate peace treaty with East Germany the following December. "It will be a cold winter," President Kennedy warned. That August the East Germans sealed off West Berlin by building their notorious wall.

UNITED PRESS INTERNATIONAL

RICHARD M. NIXON

Because of his youth, experience, oratorical ability, and California residence, Richard Milhous Nixon was an ideal running mate for Dwight D. Eisenhower in 1952. And so, just after his fortieth birthday, Nixon became the second-highest official in the federal government. Born in Yorba Linda, California, in 1913, he had graduated from Whittier College in 1934 and from Duke University Law School in 1937. After serving in the Navy during World War II, he entered California politics and was elected to the House of Representatives in 1946. He gained prominence as a member of the Committee on Un-American Activities and was elevated to the Senate in 1950. Opponents criticized Nixon's tactics, and Adlai Stevenson described him as "the kind of politician who would cut down a redwood tree, then mount the stump and make a speech for conservation." But Ike called Nixon "a courageous and honest man," and because of Eisenhower's several illnesses, the Californian became the most active Vice President up to that time. Nixon was the logical choice for the Republican presidential nomination in 1960, but John F. Kennedy outshone him in a series of televised debates and narrowly defeated him in the election. Nixon also lost a gubernatorial contest in California in 1962, but he remained a favorite of Republicans and was nominated for the Presidency again in 1968.

President Kennedy, above with President Adolfo Lopez Mateos of Mexico, was greeted with enthusiasm in Mexico City during his 1962 visit. Latin-American attitudes toward the United States were improving rapidly.

The 1961 visit to Europe also included stops in London and in Paris, where Jacqueline Kennedy dazzled even the austere General de Gaulle. Noting the press coverage given his wife, Kennedy introduced himself at a Paris luncheon as "the man who accompanied Jacqueline Kennedy to Paris. . . ."

Despite setbacks abroad, John F. Kennedy continued to push for progress at home. In 1961 and 1962 he announced plans for a national program to combat mental retardation, vigorously backed a trade expansion act, forced the steel industry to back down on a price increase, and pledged a reduction in taxes to boost the economy.

Sensitive to the narrowness of his own victory two years earlier, Kennedy campaigned exhaustively in the 1962 congressional elections. And the Democrats made the best mid-term showing since 1934 for a party in power, winning four Senate seats and losing only two in the House. Happily for Kennedy, the election followed his finest moment in office, the October, 1962, Cuban Missile Crisis.

During the early autumn, it had become evident to American intelligence that Fidel Castro was strengthening his ties to the Soviet Union. Aerial photos taken by a U-2 reconnaissance plane on Sunday, October 14, revealed that the Russians were installing offensive missiles on the island, only ninety miles off the Florida coast. There were two extreme choices open to the President: an aerial strike that would eliminate the missile threat but would risk nuclear war with Russia, or passive acceptance of the Russian challenge. Kennedy declined to consider either.

In a series of agonizing conferences over the next ten days, Kennedy and his associates reached a brilliant compromise: a naval quarantine of the island that would prevent further Soviet supplies from reaching Cuba, and a pledge that the United States would not invade if the Russians promised to dismantle and remove the missiles already there. A formula was found to allow the overextended Khrushchev to save face, and the crisis was resolved in America's favor. John F. Kennedy had demonstrated to his nation and the world the maturity and strength of the New Frontier.

In the aftermath of Cuba, Kennedy moved rapidly for a new understanding with the Soviet Union. In July, 1963, a nuclear

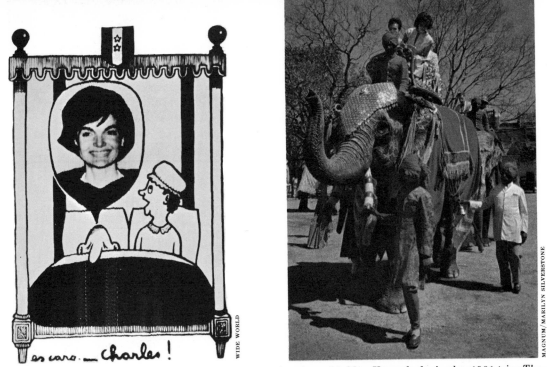

es caro. — Charles!

As the French cartoon (left) suggests, De Gaulle was quite taken with Mrs. Kennedy during her 1961 trip. The next year the First Lady and her sister, Princess Lee Radziwill, went to India and rode an elephant (right).

test ban treaty was concluded with Russia and Great Britain. The hot line, providing instant communication with the Kremlin, was installed in the White House during that summer, and in October Kennedy authorized the sale of United States surplus wheat to the Russians.

The most persistent and nettlesome domestic problem facing Kennedy during his three years in office was that of civil rights. Not strongly committed to the issue during his congressional days, Kennedy, as President, saw the demand of Negroes for equal rights as only one of his many domestic concerns. He made a conscious effort to appoint qualified Negroes to federal jobs at high levels. But he did not press for creation of a federal Department of Housing and Urban Development after it became known that Southerners would oppose the appointment of Robert C. Weaver, a Negro, as the new department's Secretary. Courting Negro votes during the 1960 campaign, Kennedy had said that it would take only the "stroke of a pen" to issue an Executive Order against racial discrimination in federal housing; in office, it took him twenty-two months to make that pen stroke. Feeling that uni-

versal suffrage was the key to Negro progress, he urged Attorney General Robert Kennedy, his brother, to intervene throughout the South in voting cases.

In September, 1962, Kennedy was compelled to send federal marshals to enforce a court order admitting James Meredith to the University of Mississippi. When violence erupted on the campus, the President federalized the National Guard and moved regular troops into the state. Negro demonstrations in 1963 further forced Kennedy's hand. In April local authorities in Birmingham, Alabama, used fire hoses and police dogs to break up civil rights marches, and the President again sent in federal troops. In the following months he helped achieve the peaceful integration of the University of Alabama, endorsed the impressive March on Washington by two hundred and fifty thousand civil rights advocates, and pressed for passage of the most comprehensive civil rights law in the nation's history (up to that time). In November, 1963, the bill passed its first important hurdle when the House Judiciary Committee reported it favorably.

That same month, far across the globe in South Vietnam, the assassination of Pres-

1005

ident Ngo Dinh Diem revealed to Kennedy once more the unending complexities of America's foreign relations. Only the preceding spring Secretary of Defense Robert McNamara had announced that the United States had "turned the corner" in its efforts to bolster the South Vietnamese regime against communism, but it now appeared that the war was entering a dangerous phase.

As 1963 drew to a close, Kennedy was faced with many problems, not the least of which was the need to build his political strength before the presidential election of November, 1964. In September he had made a highly successful "nonpolitical" tour to eleven Western states; by early November he had carried the message of his administration's accomplishments and aspirations to Massachusetts, Maine, New York, Pennsylvania, and Florida. There was special need for him to repair political fences in Texas, and he scheduled for late November a trip that would take him to San Antonio, Houston, Austin, Fort Worth, and Dallas.

In August, Mrs. Kennedy had given birth to a boy who had died of respiratory ailments thirty-nine hours later, and since then she had been convalescing. But she decided to accompany her husband to Texas.

A brash, rapidly expanding city, Dallas had a reputation for violence and extremism. The right-wing political groups in the city openly expressed their hatred of President Kennedy and his liberal policies. In 1960 Lyndon Johnson and his wife had been spat upon during a campaign appearance in the city; in October, 1963, United Nations Ambassador Adlai Stevenson, after having been vilified by demonstrators and hit with a sign in Dallas, had warned that the President might not be safe there. During Stevenson's visit Kennedy's picture had appeared on posters marked "Wanted for Treason." On November 21, the day before John F. Kennedy's arrival, a columnist for the Dallas *Morning News* wrote ominously, if flippantly, about the possibility of someone's letting go "with a broadside of grape shot in the presidential rigging if he spoke about Cuba, civil rights, taxes, or Vietnam."

On Thursday, November 21, the Kennedys received warm welcomes at San Antonio, Houston, and, late that night, Fort Worth. At noon the following day they stepped out of the presidential airplane, *Air Force One*, into warm sunshine at Dallas' Love Field. In an open limousine, the Kennedys rode with Governor and Mrs. John B. Connally. "You certainly can't say that the people of Dallas haven't given you a nice welcome," Mrs. Connally turned to say to the Kennedys. Moments later, at approximately 12:30 P.M., the car passed by the Texas School Book Depository, where—Dallas police later said—Lee Harvey Oswald waited with a rifle at a sixth-floor window.

A first bullet pierced the President's neck; a second shattered his brain. Rushed to Parkland Hospital, Kennedy was declared dead shortly after 1 P.M.

For most of the next horrifying four days, millions around the globe sat, stunned and saddened, by their radios and television sets to listen to and watch the final scenes of the meaningless tragedy. Oswald was apprehended, and on Sunday, November 24, in front of millions watching on television, was killed by Dallas night-club owner Jack Ruby.

World leaders and royalty came to Washington for the somber state funeral on Monday. But the most commanding presence that day was the black-shrouded widow, who conducted herself with unflinching dignity during the harrowing hours of the procession from the White House, the funeral mass, the burial on a hillside at Arlington National Cemetery, the lighting of the eternal flame over her husband's grave, and the reception later for the visiting dignitaries.

"I don't think there's any point in being Irish if you don't know that the world is going to break your heart eventually," Assistant Secretary of Labor Daniel P. Moynihan remarked at the time of the assassination. "I guess that we thought we had a little more time. . . . Mary McGrory said to me that we'll never laugh again. And I said, 'Heavens, Mary. We'll laugh again. It's just that we'll never be young again.' "

—JOSEPH L. GARDNER

John F. Kennedy (signature)

A PICTURE PORTFOLIO

This 1960 campaign button reflects the enormous popularity of John F. Kennedy among young Americans.

COMPETITIVENESS
AND AMBITION

Second best," Joseph Patrick Kennedy frequently reminded his family, "is a loser." The spirited competitiveness that he instilled in each of his four sons would, Joe Kennedy hoped, be applied to politics, that most competitive of activities. His own father, and his wife's, had been major figures in the Irish clique that ran Boston; he had earned a fortune great enough to make all his nine children independently wealthy, and his sons would therefore be able to rise to much greater heights than their grandfathers had. Joe, Jr., seemed the most likely to transform his father's dreams into reality. He was a top scholar, a splendid athlete, and—when Mr. Kennedy was away—the totalitarian leader of the clan. Smaller, not as strong or good-looking but just as hardheaded, John Kennedy resented having to match his brother's achievements and often did not try. As he followed Joe through private schools on the inevitable road to Choate and Harvard, he was an indifferent student and sportsman. He even attended Princeton University briefly before he finally entered Harvard. When the United States entered World War II, Joe, Jr., became a flyer and was killed; Jack went to sea and became a hero and the new focal point of the Kennedys' ambitions.

COURTESY OF MRS. JOSEPH KENNEDY

In the 1921 photograph above, Mrs. Rose Kennedy (daughter of politician John "Honey Fitz" Fitzgerald, once the mayor of Boston) poses outdoors with her family. Eunice, Kathleen, and Rosemary are by their mother; four-year-old John Fitzgerald Kennedy is sitting on the kiddy car and Joe, Jr., stands beside him.

At the age of ten, John Kennedy (above) was a good, but not outstanding, football player for the Dexter School.

The picture below was taken at an American Embassy party in London when Joseph P. Kennedy was United States ambassador. Jack was then twenty-one years old.

Navy Lieutenant (j.g.) Kennedy, above, used his father's political influence uniquely— to get him away from a desk and into action.

Afternoon teas, hostessed by Kennedy's sisters and mother, began when J. F. K. was a candidate for Congress (above) and were a part of all his later campaigns. Elected to the Senate in 1952, Kennedy was one of Washington's most eligible bachelors until September 12, 1953, when he married Jacqueline Bouvier (below).

ON THE RISE

Candidate for Congress John F. Kennedy had looks, brains, money, a well-known name, and—most necessary of all in 1946—a heroic war record. (As commander of an ill-fated PT boat in the Pacific, he had saved the lives of several of his men.) Running on that record he won handsomely. After six years in the House of Representatives, he set his sights on a higher prize—the Senate seat of Henry Cabot Lodge II. In addition to his own family name, which was more famous in Massachusetts than Kennedy's, Lodge had Dwight Eisenhower's immense popularity working for him, for he was Ike's campaign manager. Nevertheless Kennedy won; and four years, one marriage, two back operations, and one prize-winning book later, he sought the 1956 Democratic vice presidential nomination. He failed to get it, but set his sights on 1960.

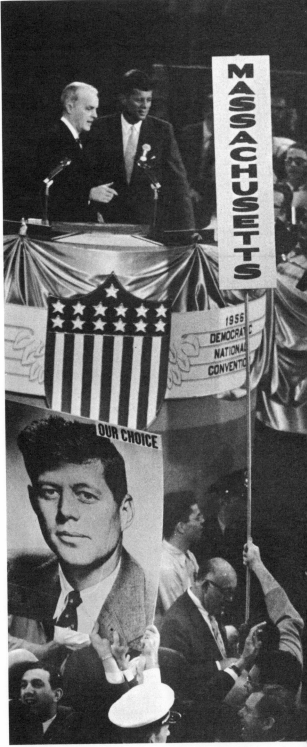

Adlai Stevenson, the 1956 Democratic presidential nominee, left the selection of a running mate to the convention delegates. On the third ballot, Senator Estes Kefauver defeated John Kennedy. That Kennedy (at right with Chairman Paul Butler) did so well was remarkable, for he would not have balanced the ticket. Even his campaign button (above), which recalled the title of his book, was a reminder of his similarities to the urbane, articulate Stevenson. Estes Kefauver, who was Southern and folksy, seemed likely to draw more votes for the Democrats.

WIDE WORLD

RUNNING HARD

The barriers blocking John Kennedy's way to the 1960 Democratic nomination and to the Presidency itself were formidable. His wealth undoubtedly helped him overcome them, but it was also held against him. If his father had influence, he also had enemies. Kennedy was young, and a Roman Catholic, and he lacked the backing of the party leaders. But evasiveness was never a Kennedy characteristic, and the candidate faced the roadblocks as they came. He reduced fears that a Catholic could not be elected President by winning the primary in West Virginia, where his religion, wealth, and Boston accent were considered serious detriments. Just before the convention, he replied to charges that he was too young by pointing out that he was older than Thomas Jefferson had been when he wrote the Declaration of Independence, than George Washington had been when he commanded the Continental Army, than Columbus had been when he discovered America. After winning the nomination, Kennedy placed religious bigots on the defensive, complimented the voters with a high-level, gimmick-free campaign, and dispelled the myth of his immaturity in a series of televised debates with his opponent, Vice President Richard M. Nixon. When Nixon criticized Harry Truman's use of profanity in a campaign speech, Kennedy added his own censure. "I have sent him," Kennedy said, "the following wire. 'Dear Mr. President: I have noted with interest your suggestion as to where those who vote for my opponent should go. While I understand and sympathize with your deep motivation, I think it is important that our side try to refrain from raising the religious issue.'"

Top: during the presidential campaign of 1960, enthusiastic Kennedy supporters (some too young to vote) press forward, hoping to touch the candidate. Kennedy's impressive performance in the televised debates with Nixon (right) won him votes, but he was elected President by a very narrow margin.

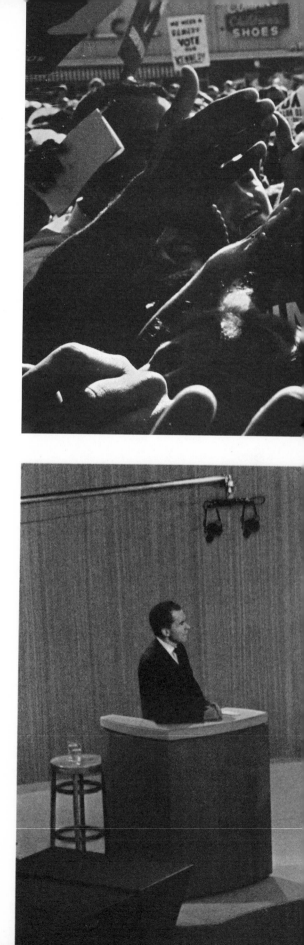

MEN OF THE NEW FRONTIER

ROBERT F. KENNEDY

Thirty-six-year-old Robert F. Kennedy, brother of the President-elect, seemed to many Americans a poor choice for Attorney General; even Bobby thought the appointment ill-advised, but he gave in to the urgings of his brother and father. "I see nothing wrong," quipped J. F. K., amidst the storm of protest, "with giving Robert some legal experience as Attorney General before he goes out to practice law." Educated at Harvard and the University of Virginia Law School, Robert Kennedy worked as a lawyer in government after completing his education, taking time out to supervise his brother's campaigns. He had been a counsel for the McCarthy committee in 1953, but had resigned in protest against its excesses and had become counsel for the committee's Democratic minority. He had been counsel for the Senate Rackets Committee and in that capacity had begun a long fight with Teamster's Union boss James Hoffa. Kennedy proved to be an able head of the Justice Department and was his brother's most trusted adviser. After J. F. K.'s assassination, Robert served in Johnson's Cabinet until 1964, when he left to run successfully for the Senate. An outspoken critic of Johnson's Vietnam policy, he was campaigning for the presidential nomination when he was assassinated on June 5, 1968.

W. AVERELL HARRIMAN

Would not naming elder statesman Averell Harriman to a post in the Kennedy administration, Robert Kennedy wanted to know, "be just an act of sentiment?" Sentimental or not, the appointment paid dividends: Harriman served first as an effective roving ambassador, then as assistant secretary of state for Far Eastern affairs and as under secretary for political affairs. In 1965 Lyndon Johnson reappointed him ambassador at large, employing Harriman's diplomatic skills wherever they were needed. Born in 1891, Harriman was educated at Groton and Yale, and inherited millions of dollars from his father, a Republican, at the age of seventeen. In 1928 he became a Democrat and subsequently held a number of important posts. Developing into a top-flight diplomat during the Roosevelt and Truman administrations, Harriman unsuccessfully sought the Democratic presidential nomination in 1952 and 1956. He was governor of New York for one term, but was defeated for re-election by Nelson Rockefeller in 1958. Although he was almost seventy and hard of hearing, his greatest service to his country was still ahead of him: in 1963 he was sent to Russia to work out a nuclear test ban treaty. In 1968 Lyndon B. Johnson named him to head the American delegation at the Vietnam peace talks in Paris.

ARTHUR J. GOLDBERG

ROBERT S. McNAMARA

In less than five years, the energetic and highly respected Arthur J. Goldberg held three of the nation's most important offices. John F. Kennedy appointed him Secretary of Labor, then associate justice of the Supreme Court; under Lyndon Johnson, Goldberg was named to succeed Adlai Stevenson as United States ambassador to the United Nations. Raised on Chicago's West Side, the youngest of eight children of Russian immigrant parents, he went to work as a delivery boy in a shoe factory when he was twelve years old. He studied at public schools and at a junior college in Chicago, then worked his way through Northwestern University, which awarded him his doctorate of jurisprudence in 1930. By the late 1930's he had begun handling law cases for labor unions, and after serving during World War II in the Office of Strategic Services, he became a leading labor lawyer. Through his work on labor legislation Goldberg met John F. Kennedy, then the junior senator from Massachusetts, and later served as a Kennedy adviser during the 1960 presidential campaign. As Secretary of Labor, Goldberg mediated a number of important labor disputes before he was appointed to the High Court in 1962. His liberal record and his reputation as a skilled bargainer led to his U.N. post, which he held for three years.

Robert Strange McNamara has been called the first truly effective Secretary of Defense. Applying to his job new techniques of management, he brought his department under strict civilian control. He led in the diversification of American weapons and military techniques, which resulted in the abandonment of dependence on nuclear weapons and gave Presidents new alternatives to draw upon in times of crisis. Born in 1916, McNamara graduated from the University of California and Harvard Business School, taught at Harvard, served as a statistician for the Air Force in World War II, and became a Ford Motor Company "Whiz Kid" in 1946. Fifteen years later, having been president of Ford for one month, McNamara was asked to take charge of the Defense Department for President John F. Kennedy. On the New Frontier, and later in the Great Society, his hardheadedness and abilities were much admired. The praise was not, however, universal. Some hawkish critics felt that McNamara had opposed rapid escalation of the war in Vietnam, while some doves held the Secretary responsible for the continuance of the fighting there. President Johnson, however, said, "I thank God every night for Bob McNamara." Early in 1968, Secretary McNamara left the Johnson Cabinet to become head of the World Bank.

Years of turmoil had made Laos a tinderbox, but in Vienna in 1961 Kennedy and Nikita Khrushchev (above) agreed to support its neutralization. Below, Kennedy explains the details at a press conference.

NIST REBEL AREAS
MARCH 1961

NORTH VIETNAM
• HANOI

PLAINE DES JARRES

Gulf of Tonkin

IENTIANE
KAM KEUT

ND

S. VIET N

(TED)

A BEGINNING

As he confessed in his Inaugural Address, President Kennedy did not expect to achieve the real and lasting peace that had eluded the world for so long. He did, however, mean to begin. The ill-fated Bay of Pigs invasion was a disastrous start, but afterward people abroad began to notice that American foreign policy was indeed changing. The old cold-war clichés were disappearing. The support that used to go to any Latin-American government that called itself anti-Communist—no matter how totalitarian—could no longer be expected, as Kennedy led the hemisphere into an Alliance for Progress, an effort to strengthen democracy in the Americas. The President could be tough, but he was willing to work with Nikita Khrushchev and did, seeking new formulas for peace and hoping to bring about a nuclear test ban treaty. When internal conflicts in Southeast Asia threatened to erupt into a major war, Kennedy rejected the assumption that neutral nations were anti-American and reversed the trend in Cambodia and in Laos. Times were still tense, but foreign skeptics, who were convinced that the United States did nothing selflessly, were confounded by the Peace Corps, which added helping hands to helping dollars, exemplified the new American attitude, and carried the spirit of the new young leader of the United States everywhere.

MAGNUM/CORNELL CAPA

THE PEACE CORPS

President Kennedy often spoke of the idealism of a "new generation of Americans." The Peace Corps put that idealism to work. Originally suggested by Senators Hubert Humphrey and Richard Neuberger in the 1950's, the corps was established by Kennedy, who became closely associated with its purpose. The young volunteer above, serving in Chimbote, Peru, built the school in which he taught.

In 1962 Mrs. Kennedy (above in the East Room) conducted a televised tour of the White House and explained her redecorating. The Bellangé chair (above right) is one of the Monroe administration pieces that the First Lady found and returned to the Mansion. She was especially proud of the redecorated Red Room (below).

THE KENNEDY STYLE

Whatever their politics, most Americans enjoyed having a stylish First Family. The Kennedys were unique: he was the youngest man ever elected to the Presidency and she was the youngest and prettiest and most elegant First Lady in modern times; their two children—Caroline and "John-John"—were unabashed scene stealers. As the average age of Americans dipped lower and lower—soon a majority would be under twenty-five years old—the nation enjoyed watching a President who had wanted the job, who had worked to get it, and who loved having it. Kennedy was not the reluctant Dwight D. Eisenhower, nor the shocked Harry S. Truman. (Roosevelt, like J. F. K., had sought the office in 1932, but that was too far back for most Americans to remember.) The whole tone—the "style"—of the White House was sharper and livelier than it had been in years. Mrs. Kennedy dug into White House history, searched the Mansion's storerooms, and redecorated the presidential home beautifully. Far from ignoring the demonstrators who appeared in front of the White House periodically, President Kennedy sent them coffee. One such demonstrator, a nuclear scientist with a "Ban the bomb" placard, was later invited to the Kennedys' dinner for American Nobel Prize winners. Robert Frost read one of his poems at the inauguration and W. H. Auden, Robert Lowell, and John Steinbeck sat on the rostrum. On another occasion, Pablo Casals played at a White House concert. There were cynics and critics, but Thornton Wilder said that Kennedy was creating "a whole new world of surprised self-respect" in the arts. "It is a good thing," Ernest Hemingway wrote, "to have a brave man as our President in times as tough as these are. . . ." Said Steinbeck, "What a joy that literacy is no longer prima-facie evidence of treason."

CECIL STOUGHTON

Above: President and Mrs. Kennedy congratulate virtuoso cellist Pablo Casals after a White House concert.

JIMMY SCOTT/COURTESY OF *Topaz*, SANTIAGO, CHILE

U.S. SIGNAL CORPS

If Castro was, as the cartoon above implies, the creator of the 1962 Missile Crisis, he was also its main casualty. Clearly, Kennedy could not tolerate Soviet missiles in Cuba, and Khrushchev was not going to risk war to give Castro the "protection" he claimed American intentions warranted.

The huge crowd that welcomed J. F. K. to Berlin (top right) in 1963 became hysterical when he said, "All free men . . . are citizens of Berlin." In contrast, the civil rights marchers who converged on Washington (right) were quite restrained. But the whole country was impressed.

MAGNUM/CHARLES HARBUTT

COMMITMENT

In terms of tangible accomplishments, the first twenty months of the Kennedy administration had been unexceptional. In a subtler way, however, the period had been remarkable: the relationship between the people and the government had been re-established. Prodded by the President, the young and not so young became involved with issues; *commitment* was their watchword. This was important groundwork for Kennedy, who hoped to make 1963 a year of calculable achievement. It began, however, in the shadow of the Cuban Missile Crisis. In October, 1962, the President had insisted that Russia remove the missiles it had installed in Cuba and had ordered a blockade of the island. Kennedy was firm and the Russians complied, but because the President had also been restrained, the talks that led to the nuclear test ban treaty of 1963 were able to continue. That Kennedy had emerged as an international leader became apparent during his European trip as he was welcomed warmly in city after city. At home, responding to the brutality with which the American Negro's demand for equality was resisted, Kennedy said that civil rights was "a moral issue" and asked Congress to pass the strongest civil rights bill in history.

His reaction to crowds revealed much about the President. When a quarter of a million black and white Americans marched peacefully on Washington in August, 1963, he was proud—although the participants were by no means uniformly pro-Kennedy. When three-fifths of Berlin's people welcomed him with unrestrained enthusiasm, he was disturbed: he felt the crowd was hysterical, irrational. Best of all John F. Kennedy liked the reception he received in Ireland, where he recited an old Irish song: "Come back around to the land of thy birth./Come with the shamrock in the springtime. . . ." "This is not," he confessed, "the land of my birth, but . . . I certainly will come back in the springtime."

1021

ADMIRED AMERICANS

ALL: WIDE WORLD

RALPH J. BUNCHE

'To most whites," wrote Simeon Booker in *Black Man's America*, "United Nations Under Secretary Ralph J. Bunche symbolizes the successful and prominent Negro." More than a symbol of Negro success, Dr. Bunche is one of America's most highly respected international spokesmen. The grandson of a Southern slave, Bunche was born in Detroit, Michigan, in 1904 and was educated at the University of California and at Harvard, where he received an M.A. and a Ph.D. In 1928 he began teaching political science at Harvard University. Later he assisted Gunnar Myrdal in producing a study of the Negro's problems, *An American Dilemma*, published in 1944. During World War II Bunche served the government as an adviser on Africa, and in 1944 he joined the State Department as an expert on Africa and dependent territories. After attending several international conferences for the planning of the United Nations, he joined the United Nations Secretariat in 1946 as the director of the Trusteeship Division. Appointed mediator of the Arab-Israeli dispute in 1948, he was awarded the Nobel Peace Prize in 1950 for his successful negotiation of an armistice. As United Nations under secretary for special political affairs after 1957, he continued to win acclaim, particularly for his work in the underdeveloped nations of Africa and the Middle East.

HELEN KELLER

"The marvelous richness of human experience would lose something of rewarding joy," wrote Helen Keller, "if there were no limitations to overcome." In her triumph over her handicaps, Miss Keller became a source of inspiration to millions. Born in Alabama in 1880, she was stricken when she was nineteen months old with an illness described as brain fever. Left blind and deaf, she spent her childhood in inarticulate frustration until, when she was seven, her parents sent for a teacher, Anne Sullivan, from the Perkins Institute of the Blind. Within a few weeks Miss Sullivan, using the manual alphabet, penetrated the darkness surrounding the child's brilliant mind. Standing by the well pump one day as her teacher spelled the word "w-a-t-e-r" on her palm, Helen suddenly comprehended the meaning of language. Thereafter, she quickly learned to read Braille, to write, and even to speak. With Miss Sullivan spelling out the lectures, Miss Keller studied at Radcliffe College, from which she graduated *cum laude* in 1904. She subsequently devoted her life to helping the handicapped as an essayist, lecturer, educator, and international counselor. She also wrote several remarkable books. Her early life was dramatized in a popular play, *The Miracle Worker*. "Life," Miss Keller believed, "is either a daring adventure or nothing." She died in 1968 at eighty-seven.

JONAS E. SALK

JOHN GLENN

The announcement of Dr. Jonas E. Salk's antipolio vaccine in 1953 was hailed as a medical milestone. "If the vaccine fulfills the hope that at last a way has been found to cope with poliomyelitis," reported *The New York Times*, ". . . Dr. Salk will have scored one of the greatest triumphs in the history of medicine." Dr. Salk had begun his work on viral diseases in 1938 as a medical student at New York University. Continuing his research at the University of Michigan from 1942 to 1947, he won recognition for his work on influenza vaccines. In 1947 he moved to the University of Pittsburgh, where he began his research on a polio vaccine. After growing the polio virus in the nonnervous tissues of monkey kidneys and then killing the virus with formaldehyde, Dr. Salk showed the killed-virus vaccine to be effective in producing antibodies against the disease. Following a carefully controlled test on more than a million children in 1954, the Salk vaccine was found to be "safe, effective, and potent." By 1961 the incidence of polio in the United States had been reduced by 96 per cent, and subsequently the crippling disease, which in 1952 had afflicted 57,626 persons (mostly children), ceased to be a major threat. Dr. Salk, who was awarded a medal by Congress, continued his research as director of the Salk Institute for Biological Studies in California.

On February 20, 1962, Lieutenant Colonel John H. Glenn, Jr., became the first American to orbit the earth. In history's third orbital space flight (following two by Russian cosmonauts in 1961), Glenn lifted off from Cape Canaveral, Florida, circled the world three times in his Mercury space capsule (the *Friendship 7*), and splashed down in the Atlantic Ocean—all within less than five hours. Americans were elated. As a friend of Colonel Glenn's remarked, "With the nuclear anxiety and the Russian supremacy in space we needed a man to make us all feel proud again. John Glenn has always had that quality." Born in Cambridge, Ohio, in 1921, Glenn became a Marine Corps aviator in 1943. He flew one hundred forty-nine missions during World War II and the Korean conflict, and received five Distinguished Flying Crosses. In 1954 Glenn became a test pilot. He made the first supersonic flight from Los Angeles to New York in 1957, and two years later was one of seven men chosen for the government's man-in-space program. After suborbital flights by fellow astronauts Alan Shepard and Virgil Grissom in 1961, Glenn made the first American orbital flight the next year. In 1964 he left the space program to return to Ohio and enter the senatorial race there, but a severe ear injury forced him to withdraw. Colonel Glenn was subsequently employed in private industry.

The President was killed and Texas Governor John Connally (above left in the car with the Kennedys) was wounded when an assassin fired at their motorcade in Dallas. In the blurred picture above—one frame of an amateur's movie film—Mrs. Kennedy climbs on the trunk of the car to help a Secret Service man aboard just after the shots. Right: the Kennedy family and the Johnsons after a service at the Capitol in Washington.

DAYS OF MOURNING

He died of exposure," wrote E. B. White just after President Kennedy was killed in Dallas, "but in a way that he would have settled for—in the line of duty, and with his friends and enemies all around, supporting him and shooting at him." Grief settled in places that would have surprised even Kennedy. Bells rang in London, dirges were played on Russian radios, and Charles de Gaulle was "stunned" that his people were weeping, "as though he were a Frenchman, a member of their own family." A native in Africa walked ten miles through the bush to tell the American consul, "I have lost a friend and I am so sorry." Americans were numb, disbelieving, and angry—not just at Lee Harvey Oswald, who had been arrested for the assassination, but even at the dead President. "He did not fear the weather . . ." White wrote, "but instead challenged the wind itself," and although the people admired that in him, they did not see why he had felt compelled to challenge the Dallas winds. "Nut country" the President had called it, but he went anyway and was killed.

He was buried three days later, and the traditional riderless horse that followed the coffin to the grave might have been created for this one awful day. He side-stepped and tossed his handsome head back and snorted and pulled, reluctant to go, his very determination and independence symbolizing the spirit of the fallen leader.

In the months that followed, John Kennedy was idolized and minimized. His place in history was argued about because making a country young again—giving it vigor—is a hard thing to measure. "For a time," writer Norman Mailer said, "we felt the country was ours. Now it's theirs again."

On November 25, the four dark days that began with the shooting of the President came to a close. At left, the funeral procession moves toward Arlington Cemetery, where John F. Kennedy was interred.

FACTS IN SUMMARY: JOHN F. KENNEDY

CHRONOLOGY

UNITED STATES		KENNEDY
U.S. enters World War I	1917	Born May 29
Stock market crash	1929	
Franklin D. Roosevelt elected President	1932	
WPA created / Social Security established	1935	Graduates from the Choate School / Studies at London School of Economics / Attends Princeton briefly
	1936	Enters Harvard
Roosevelt attempts to pack Supreme Court	1937	
	1938	Serves in London as secretary to his father
France falls to Germans	1940	Graduates from Harvard / Publishes Why England Slept
Pearl Harbor attacked / Germany and Italy declare war on U.S.	1941	Appointed ensign in Naval Reserve
Battle of Bataan / Battle of Midway	1942	Assigned to Motor Torpedo Boat Squadron
Sicily and Italy invaded / U.S. offensive in Central Pacific	1943	Sent to South Pacific / PT-109 sunk by Japanese destroyer / Returns to U.S. because of back injury and malaria
U.S. takes Marshall and Mariana islands / Allies land in France / Philippines Campaign begins / Battle of the Bulge	1944	Undergoes disc operation / Joseph Kennedy, Jr., killed in action
Yalta Conference / Roosevelt dies / Truman becomes President / V-E Day / U.N. organized / Potsdam Conference / First atomic bomb dropped on Hiroshima / V-J Day	1945	Employed by International News Service / Covers U.N. conference / Covers Potsdam Conference
War crimes trials held at Nuremberg	1946	Elected to House of Representatives
Truman Doctrine / Marshall Plan / Taft-Hartley Act	1947	Votes against Taft-Hartley Act
Berlin Airlift begins / Truman elected President	1948	Re-elected to House of Representatives
NATO pact signed / Russia explodes atomic bomb / Nationalist Chinese evacuate mainland	1949	Fights for federal aid to housing / Criticizes Truman's China policy
Korean War begins	1950	Re-elected to House of Representatives
First U.S. H-bomb test / Eisenhower elected President	1952	Defeats Henry Cabot Lodge in race for Senate
Stalin dies / Armistice in Korea / Russia explodes H-bomb	1953	Marries Jacqueline Bouvier
Supreme Court desegregation order / Army-McCarthy hearings	1954	Undergoes spinal-fusion operation / Fails to pair on McCarthy censure
	1955	Undergoes second back operation
Hungarian Revolt / Eisenhower re-elected President	1956	Publishes Profiles in Courage / Almost nominated for Vice President / Campaigns for Stevenson
Civil Rights Act / Little Rock school integration crisis / Russians orbit Sputnik I	1957	Supports Civil Rights Act / Profiles in Courage wins Pulitzer Prize
First U.S. satellite orbited	1958	Re-elected to Senate
Fidel Castro comes to power in Cuba	1959	Begins campaign for Presidency
U-2 shot down in Russia	1960	Wins primaries in New Hampshire, Wisconsin, and West Virginia / Elected President
Eisenhower breaks off diplomatic relations with Cuba / Russian cosmonaut Gagarin becomes first man to enter space / Invasion of Cuba by U.S.-supported exiles fails / Astronauts Shepard and Grissom make sub-orbital space flights / Berlin Wall built	1961	Inaugurated as President / Acts to brake recession and outflow of gold / Announces formation of Peace Corps / Announces Alliance for Progress in Latin America / Accepts blame for Bay of Pigs debacle / Moves to neutralize Laos / Confers with De Gaulle, Khrushchev, and Macmillan in Europe / Suggests "peace race" in U.N. speech / Declares continued U.S. support for Vietnam independence

	1962	
Lt. Col. Glenn in first U.S. orbital space flight	1962	*Asks for U.S.-Russian cooperation in space exploration*
Steel prices raised, then lowered		*Orders resumption of U.S. nuclear tests*
Geneva Conference ensures neutral Laos		*Forces steel companies to retract price increase*
Riots on University of Mississippi campus over admission of Negro		*Sends federal troops to University of Mississippi*
Soviet missile build-up in Cuba		*Campaigns in mid-term congressional elections*
Trade Expansion Act		*Meets Russian missile threat in Cuba with quarantine*
Democrats gain four Senate seats, lose two House seats in mid-term elections		*Orders end to racial discrimination in federal housing*
Major Cooper orbits earth twenty-two times	1963	*Sends federal troops to quiet Birmingham race riots*
Limited nuclear test ban treaty signed by U.S., U.S.S.R., and Great Britain		*Aids peaceful integration of University of Alabama*
March on Washington, D.C., by civil rights supporters		*Suggests combining of U.S. and Soviet efforts for moon exploration*
Stevenson abused during visit to Dallas		*Approves sale of wheat to Russia*
Armed forces coup in South Vietnam		*Assassinated in Dallas, November 22*

JACQUES LOWE

Kennedy and his family, during the campaign of 1960

BIOGRAPHICAL FACTS

BIRTH: Brookline, Mass., May 29, 1917

ANCESTRY: Irish

FATHER: Joseph Patrick Kennedy; b. East Boston, Mass., Sept. 6, 1888

FATHER'S OCCUPATIONS: Financier; diplomat

MOTHER: Rose Fitzgerald Kennedy; b. Boston, Mass., 1891

BROTHERS: Joseph Patrick (1915–1944); Robert Francis (1925–1968); Edward Moore (1932–   )

SISTERS: Rosemary (1919–   ); Kathleen (1920–1948); Eunice Mary (1921–   ); Patricia (1924–   ); Jean Ann (1928–   )

WIFE: Jacqueline Lee Bouvier; b. Southampton, N.Y., July 28, 1929

MARRIAGE: Newport, R.I., Sept. 12, 1953

CHILDREN: Caroline Bouvier (1957–   ); John Fitzgerald (1960–   ); Patrick Bouvier (1963)

EDUCATION: Attended the Choate School; London School of Economics; Princeton University; graduated from Harvard University (1940); Stanford University

RELIGIOUS AFFILIATION: Roman Catholic

OCCUPATIONS BEFORE PRESIDENCY: Author; politician

MILITARY SERVICE: Ensign, lieutenant (j.g.), lieutenant, U.S. Naval Reserve (active duty 1941–1945)

PRE-PRESIDENTIAL OFFICES: Member U.S. House of Representatives; Member U.S. Senate

AGE AT INAUGURATION: 43

DEATH: Dallas, Texas, Nov. 22, 1963

PLACE OF BURIAL: Arlington National Cemetery, Arlington, Va.

ELECTION OF 1960

CANDIDATES	ELECTORAL VOTE	POPULAR VOTE
John F. Kennedy Democratic	303	34,226,731
Richard M. Nixon Republican	219	34,108,157

THE KENNEDY ADMINISTRATION

INAUGURATION: January 20, 1961; the Capitol, Washington, D.C.

VICE PRESIDENT: Lyndon B. Johnson

SECRETARY OF STATE: Dean Rusk

SECRETARY OF THE TREASURY: C. Douglas Dillon

SECRETARY OF DEFENSE: Robert S. McNamara

ATTORNEY GENERAL: Robert F. Kennedy

POSTMASTER GENERAL: J. Edward Day

SECRETARY OF THE INTERIOR: Stewart L. Udall

SECRETARY OF AGRICULTURE: Orville L. Freeman

SECRETARY OF COMMERCE: Luther H. Hodges

SECRETARY OF LABOR: Arthur J. Goldberg; W. Willard Wirtz (from Sept. 25, 1962)

SECRETARY OF HEALTH, EDUCATION, AND WELFARE: Abraham A. Ribicoff; Anthony J. Celebrezze (from July 31, 1962)

AMBASSADOR TO UNITED NATIONS: Adlai E. Stevenson

SUPREME COURT APPOINTMENTS: Byron R. White (1962); Arthur J. Goldberg (1962)

87th CONGRESS (January 3, 1961–January 3, 1963):
Senate: 65 Democrats; 35 Republicans
House: 263 Democrats; 174 Republicans

88th CONGRESS (January 3, 1963–January 3, 1965):
Senate: 67 Democrats; 33 Republicans
House: 258 Democrats; 177 Republicans

LYNDON BAINES JOHNSON

Casting a lengthening shadow over American history for more than a generation, Lyndon Baines Johnson has stood, as journalists Rowland Evans and Robert Novak have pointed out, "near or at the center of power in Washington for all the great political events of our epoch. . . . No man in American history became President with a greater relish for power or with more experience. . . ."

Few Presidents have been as controversial as L. B. J. Eastern critics have lampooned him as petulant, impetuous, and unsophisticated, as a county chairman writ large, a cloakroom Machiavelli out of his depth in the Presidency, or a covert Dixiecrat. He has been booed in Dallas as a pawn of the Yankees and accused of preaching socialism on the Texas stump. To his admirers, however, Lyndon Johnson ranks with Franklin D. Roosevelt in vision and achievement. Democratic chieftain James A. Farley says flatly that "we never had a finer leader. . . ." Johnson, writes historian A. A. Berle of Harvard, "is not a romantic image. The brilliant court and flashing pennons of Camelot are not his. . . . Rather . . . the small-farmer's son become President has plotted out in his Great Society the contours and trace-lines of the next major social development in America."

On one point Johnson's detractors and loyalists agree unconditionally: L. B. J. has brought to the White House a political genius, a technique of persuasion and direction perhaps without parallel in American history. Richard Nixon concedes that he is "one of the ablest political craftsmen of our times." Adlai Stevenson hailed Johnson's "extraordinary managerial skill" and called him "a master of the art of the possible in politics."

Of L. B. J.'s political destiny his grandfather Sam had had no doubt. When Lyndon was born to Sam, Jr., and Rebekah Baines Johnson near Stonewall,

Lyndon B. Johnson in 1964

Texas, on August 27, 1908, Sam, Sr., spread the word to all who would listen: "A United States Senator was born this morning. . . ." Politics ran on both sides of the Johnson family line. L. B. J.'s ancestors had helped settle the South, one of them having served as governor of Kentucky. His paternal grandfather, a Confederate veteran, had settled and given his name to Johnson City, Texas. Rebekah Johnson's father had served in the Texas legislature and as Texas secretary of state, and Lyndon's father was also a member of the Texas legislature.

Lyndon Johnson emerged not from the Texas of oil barons or cowboys, but from the mean, stony, drought-cursed soil of the southwest hill country. The Johnsons were not poor, but they knew hard times and scrambled for what they earned. Sam was an occasional schoolteacher and a farmer who was hard hit by the agricultural depression of the twenties. "I know that as a farm boy I did not feel secure," President Johnson recalled, "and when I was 14 years I decided I was not going to be the victim of a system which would allow the price of a commodity like cotton to drop from 40 cents to 6 cents and destroy the homes of people like my own family."

"Thin as a willow fishing pole," Lyndon at fifteen already stood more than six feet tall. For pocket money, he worked at odd jobs: picking cotton, shining shoes at the Johnson City barbershop, passing out handbills. After graduating from high school, he went west. "Up and down the coast I tramped, washing dishes, waiting on tables, doing farmwork," he recalled, ". . . and always growing thinner and more homesick." Back home, he joined a road gang and, harnessed to mules, worked a buck scraper.

Agreeing with his mother that such a life honored neither him nor his eminent forebears, Johnson entered Southwest Texas State Teachers College in San Marcos in February, 1927. He majored in history, headed the debating team, and bulldozed his way to political primacy on campus. To finance his way through college—in an accelerated course—he worked as a school jan-

Lyndon Johnson, when he was eighteen months old

itor, a secretary in the college president's office, and a teacher of Mexican-Americans. He graduated with a B.S. degree in 1930.

Immediately after college, Johnson taught public speaking at Houston's Sam Houston High School. In 1931 he campaigned hard for the election to the House of Representatives of a wealthy conservative, Richard M. Kleberg. When Kleberg won, Johnson accompanied him to Washington, where he served for four years as his secretary. Already enjoying the kindly paternal eye of his father's friend, Congressman Sam Rayburn, Johnson rapidly gained a reputation for political acuity, serving as the *de facto* leader of the Little Congress, an informal group of House secretaries.

On November 17, 1934, L. B. J., who had bought a ring for two dollars and fifty cents at Sears Roebuck, married Claudia Alta Taylor (nicknamed Lady Bird by a family cook), the daughter of a well-to-do eastern Texas landowner. She would bear him two daughters, Lynda Bird and Luci Baines.

In the spring of 1935 Johnson returned to Texas, where he served for eighteen months as state director of F. D. R.'s National Youth Administration. Under Johnson's efficient leadership, the NYA lent money to, or secured part-time employment in the construction of state parks, schools, and libraries for, an estimated seventy-five to one hundred thousand students, who were thus enabled to continue in college.

Lyndon Johnson's tenure as NYA director widened his political base in the Texas precincts. When the congressional seat in Johnson's Tenth District fell vacant early in 1937, L. B. J. threw his hat in the ring. Lumping his several conservative opponents together as an unholy alliance of "trembling, fear and reaction," Johnson equated a vote for himself with a vote for Roosevelt, espousing even F. D. R.'s ill-advised Supreme Court-packing plan. His strategy worked. On April 10 L. B. J., aged twenty-eight, was elected to Congress. The next day he met Roosevelt at Galveston and accepted F. D. R.'s invitation to accompany him across Texas. From that excursion Johnson emerged as an overt protégé of Roosevelt's. F. D. R. was responsible for Johnson's prompt appointment to the House Naval Affairs Committee. Johnson, a friend recalled, was "a real pusher . . . maybe a little too cocky . . . but he did get things done."

Johnson worked hard for his home district. He obtained millions of federal dollars for local projects and pressed successfully for rural electrification by public, rather than private, power companies. He was instrumental, too, in locating a naval air-training base in Corpus Christi and shipyards in Houston and Orange, all outside his district.

Vice President John Nance Garner's open defiance of F. D. R.'s bid for a third term in 1940 provided Johnson with another opportunity to stand up as a Roosevelt loyalist. He not only supported the President but he headed the House Democratic Congressional Campaign Committee, which was credited with averting Republican gains.

In April, 1941, L. B. J. made his first bid for a seat in the United States Senate. Announcing, from the steps of the White House, his decision to run, Johnson entered the fray against three opponents. During the campaign he strongly supported Roosevelt's program of military preparedness and his appeal for an end to isolationism. Ridiculed as a yes man, Johnson agreed: "I am a yes man," he declared, "for everything that is American." And if war should come, he pledged, and "my vote must be cast to send your boy to war, that day Lyndon Johnson will leave his seat in Congress to go with him." Johnson lost to Governor W. Lee O'Daniel by 1,311 votes. After this defeat he consciously moved to the right to consolidate his political power base in a more urban, ambitious Texas, which was dominated by conservative oil interests.

His defeat notwithstanding, Lyndon made good his pledge to leave his seat in Congress and go on active duty in the Navy. Assigned first to a post in San Francisco, he appealed to Roosevelt for a more active job. In May, 1942, Lieutenant Commander Johnson landed on New Caledonia, an island off the east coast of Australia, on a special presidential mission to assess American morale and military strength in the Pacific combat zone. In June, Johnson boarded a B-26 bomber en route from Port Moresby to a mission over the Japanese air base at Lae, near Salamaua. As the B-26 approached the target, one of its engines failed. The aircraft fell back from the bomber group, becoming an easy prey for attacking Japanese fighters. Though hit several times, Johnson's plane ducked out of range and, badly damaged, limped back to Port Moresby. For showing "marked coolness in spite of the hazard involved," L. B. J. was awarded the Silver Star Medal.

When Roosevelt ordered all congressmen serving in the armed forces to return home, Johnson assumed the chairmanship of a subcommittee of the Naval Affairs Committee; the subcommittee was charged with investigating Navy procurement procedures in order to eliminate waste. Congressman Johnson drafted the "work or fight" bill, which "froze" workers in key war positions and called for the drafting of those who would not work in war plants. He also supported the Smith-Connally antistrike act.

After V-J Day Johnson, a member of the Postwar Military Policy Committee, decried what he described as America's precipitate dismantling of its war machine and helped draft security legislation. He was also named to the Joint Committee on Atomic Energy. He approved of the controversial Taft-Hartley Act and voted to override President Truman's veto of that legislation.

In 1948 Johnson again sought a Senate seat, facing a conservative former Texas governor, Coke Stevenson, in the decisive Democratic primary. It was a virulent campaign. L. B. J. ran on a platform of preparedness, peace, and progress, urging stronger armed forces, a viable United Nations, and federal aid to Texas for soil conservation and rural electrification. Johnson also charged that the "big labor racketeers, the labor dictatorship" opposed him because he had voted for "the anti-Communist Taft-Hartley bill." Johnson—taking a position he would change in later years—attacked Truman's civil rights program as "a farce and a sham—an effort to set up a police state in the guise of liberty." He argued that his House vote against repealing the poll tax had been a defense of states' rights and said of his vote against appropriations for the Fair Employment Practices Commission: "If a man can tell you whom you must hire, he can tell you whom you can't hire."

The result of the first primary was inconclusive: Stevenson won 477,077 votes to Johnson's 405,617, while nine other candidates shared 320,000 votes. In a runoff election Johnson edged past Stevenson by a mere 87 votes. After torrid confrontations in court that are still shrouded in allegation and controversy, Johnson was certified as the Democratic candidate. He was then elected to the United States Senate by a ratio of 2 to 1.

Johnson was promptly named to the Senate Armed Services Committee, on which he pursued his central theme of military preparedness, joined Senator Stuart Symington in the latter's cold-war fight for a strengthened Air Force, and warned, in February, 1950, that the United States could no longer rely on the "security of an atomic monopoly." Johnson supported the Korean War effort, though he attacked Tru-

man's conduct of the war. He headed the Senate Preparedness Investigating Subcommittee, which fought military inefficiency and waste. He branded Truman's seizure of the steel mills "dictatorship" and voted to negate the President's veto of the McCarran-Walter Immigration Act. Conscious of his narrow victory in 1948, he mended his fences with Oil Texas and sided with the coalition of conservative Democrats and Republicans.

In the 1952 presidential campaign, Johnson supported Adlai Stevenson unenthusiastically but insisted that "the Democratic Party is best for Texas and the South and the nation." After Dwight Eisenhower's victory he said, "We have a new leader. I won't discuss the wisdom of the choice, but he is our leader. Some people have gone off into the corner to pout. Others want to tear down, but any jackass can kick down a barn. It takes a good carpenter to build a barn. We aim to build."

Most certainly Eisenhower's victory helped build Lyndon Johnson. In January, 1953, forty-four-year-old L. B. J. was elected Minority Leader of the Senate. Democrats, he announced, would not oppose for the sake of opposition. "All of us," he explained, "are Americans before we are members of any political organization." There was one major exception to his cooperation with Eisenhower. When the latter considered sending American planes to aid the beleaguered French forces at Dienbienphu in Indochina, Johnson declared that such action would place the United States "in clear danger of being left naked and alone in a hostile world. . . ." He demanded that the consent of the British be obtained before any intervention occurred. When the British turned down the proposal, the idea was abandoned.

The election of 1954, in which Johnson himself was easily re-elected, gave control of Congress to the Democrats and catapulted L. B. J. into a national prominence second only to Eisenhower's. At forty-six, Johnson was named Majority Leader of the Senate.

"I do not think it is an exaggeration to say," Walter Lippmann observed, "that Mr. Eisenhower's success as President began when the Republicans lost control of Congress and the standing committees." At no point in his career had Johnson pursued more effectively his political approach of good will: "Come now and let us reason together." He drummed up votes on both sides of the aisle for Eisenhower's Formosa Resolution, which warned Peking not to move against Taiwan; for Eisenhower's minimum-wage reform bill, topping the President's proposed ninety-cent minimum by ten cents; and for Eisenhower's Mutual Security Act and Reciprocal Trade Agreement extensions. Presidential historian Louis W. Koenig called L. B. J. "one of the most illustrious floor leaders in Senate history," a master architect of political accommodation who commanded "a relentless, overpowering persuasiveness. . . ."

Johnson's career as Majority Leader was interrupted on July 2, 1955, when he suffered a heart attack that was diagnosed as a "myocardial infarction of a moderately severe character." (L. B. J. later described the attack as being "about as bad as you can have and live.") He recovered quickly and was back in the Senate six months later.

In 1957 Johnson personally shepherded through the Senate the first civil rights bill in eighty-two years, and in 1960 guided the passage of the second, which provided new voting registration guarantees for Negroes. "More than any other politician since the Civil War," said James Reston in *The New York Times*, Johnson "has, on the race problem, been the most effective mediator between the North and the South."

When the Soviet Union rocked the United States out of its complacency by launching Sputnik I in 1957, Johnson initiated a Senate Preparedness Subcommittee investigation to find out why the Soviets had forged ahead in the space race, and again appealed for a strengthened strategic Air Force and for acceleration of America's space and missile effort. He also chaired the Senate Committee on Aeronautical and Space Sciences and helped establish NASA and the National Aeronautics and Space Council.

In June, 1957, Johnson called for "an open curtain for full discussion" between the United States and the Soviet Union. "Let the people know!" he declared. ". . . And when the people know, they will insist that

Vice President-elect Lyndon Johnson relaxes at his ranch in mid-November of 1960. L. B. J. had campaigned effectively in the South, an area of concern to Kennedy; the Republicans won only three Southern states.

Lady Bird Johnson, the energetic First Lady, visits an old Pueblo settlement at San Ildefonso, New Mexico.

the arms race, the nuclear explosions, the intercontinental missiles all be banished." In a dramatic demonstration of political unity, Johnson also appeared before the United Nations in 1958 as Eisenhower's personal envoy to plead for international cooperation in the use of outer space.

That Johnson was built of presidential timber his boosters never doubted. L. B. J. himself made behind-the-scenes soundings and permitted extensive politicking on his behalf, but he stayed out of the 1960 primaries, insisting that somebody had to "tend the store" in Washington.

At the convention Johnson had considerable delegate support. But John F. Kennedy could not be stopped despite an eleventh-hour confrontation with Johnson, in which the latter tried to ridicule Kennedy's lack of experience. On the first ballot Johnson polled 409 votes to Kennedy's winning 806.

Then, in one of the great political surprises of American history, Johnson was offered, and accepted, the vice presidential nomination. Political analysts agree that Johnson's appearance on the Democratic ticket spelled the difference between defeat and victory for John F. Kennedy, who indisputably needed Johnson to carry the South.

Vice President Johnson served as a presidential emissary abroad, making several celebrated trips. At home L. B. J. attended Cabinet sessions, served on the National Security Council, maintained a degree of liaison between the White House and Capitol Hill, and headed the National Aeronautics and Space Council, the Peace Corps Advisory Council, and the President's Committee on Equal Employment Opportunity.

The Vice Presidency was patently not compatible with Johnson's uninhibited ego, his ambition, or his phenomenal energy. Within a heartbeat of ultimate power, he exercised almost none. But on November 22, 1963, the tragedy in Dallas placed Lyndon Johnson at the summit of world power. Two hours after the assassination of John F. Kennedy, Johnson stood solemnly aboard the presidential plane, *Air Force One*, still on the ground at Dallas' Love Field, and took the oath of office as the thirty-sixth President. His oath taken and the transfer of executive power swiftly achieved, Johnson left little doubt of his determination to demonstrate that "our institutions cannot be disrupted by an assassin's bullet."

The new President spoke before a joint session of Congress on November 27. "All I have," he said, "I would have given gladly not to be standing here today." But John Kennedy's dream, he declared, would not die. Kennedy, Johnson recalled, had said, "'Let us begin.' Today in this moment of new resolve," Johnson told Congress, "I would say to all my fellow Americans, let us continue." Then Lyndon Baines Johnson, son of the South, appealed to Congress: "No memorial oration or eulogy," he declared,

An intent President Johnson watches the flight of a Saturn rocket launched at Cape Kennedy early in 1964.

"could more eloquently honor President Kennedy's memory than the earliest possible passage of the civil rights bill for which he fought so long."

In his first State of the Union message, delivered in January, 1964, President Johnson pressed the point home: "Let this session of Congress," he said, "be known as the session which did more for civil rights than the last hundred sessions combined. . . ." And in another historic departure, after renewing his appeals for medical care for the elderly and a tax cut, the President announced: "This administration today here and now declares unconditional war on poverty in America."

Johnson's skill as a legislative leader was then brought to bear upon Congress. In a rare display of bipartisan unity, the historic Eighty-eighth Congress passed the Civil Rights Act of 1964—including the public accommodations and the fair employment practices sections.

If the Civil Rights Act was the most dramatic, it was by no means the sole achievement of Johnson's first year in the White House. "Johnson had scarcely settled in office," wrote Michael Davie, "before bills were coming out of Congress like candy bars from a slot machine. . . ." Johnson asked for and got laws authorizing the tax cut requested by Kennedy; federal aid to mass transit facilities; a huge antipoverty program; and wheat and cotton price support,

including a food-stamp plan for providing food to the needy in urban areas. The Job Corps, designed to train young Americans and employ them in public projects, was also established.

Johnson's mastery of Congress and his clearly sincere determination to avoid identification with any single section or interest won him allegiance from both the business and the labor communities. When the railroad unions called a national strike for April 10, 1964, President Johnson summoned both labor and management to the White House. If both sides could not agree to a settlement that would be in the national interest, he announced, he would appeal to his overwhelmingly Democratic Congress to require compulsory arbitration of the dispute. An agreement was reached and the strike was averted. The railroad settlement epitomized the strength of the "Johnson treatment." As columnist Mary McGrory wrote, "The full treatment is an incredibly potent mixture of persuasion, badgering, flattery, threats, reminders of past favors and future advantages."

From the moment of his accession to the Presidency, Johnson labored under a great handicap. He governed in a climate of national grief and political polarities and in the shadow of a handsome young President who had enjoyed immense popularity. Johnson labored, too, under the bitter fact that Kennedy had been killed in Texas during an

Newlyweds Luci Johnson and Pat Nugent leave the Shrine of the Immaculate Conception on August 6, 1966. Lynda Bird (behind Luci) was maid of honor.

"I have come here today to make it unmistakably clear that the assassin's bullet which took [Kennedy's] life did not alter his nation's purpose," he told the world body. Johnson urged a war on hunger, poverty, and disease. "The United States wants to see the cold war end . . ." he added; "the United States wants to press on with arms control and reduction. . . ."

In the first months of his Presidency, Johnson faced new challenges in the Caribbean. When Fidel Castro demanded the return to Cuba of the United States naval base at Guantanamo and shut off the installation's water, Johnson calmly ordered the base to devise its own water supply. He also threatened to dismiss Cubans who worked on the base unless they spent their wages there. When Cuban fishing boats appeared in United States waters, they were seized. Castro turned the water back on.

Johnson acted with similar restraint when President Roberto Chiari of Panama—spurred by nationalist rioting in the Canal Zone—demanded renegotiation of the Panama Canal treaty and severed diplomatic relations with Washington. After initial pique on both sides had cooled, Johnson announced that a new treaty would be negotiated, thereby restoring United States-Panamanian relations to their traditional balance.

The one issue that overshadowed Lyndon Johnson's Presidency from the start was the war for control of South Vietnam. Indisputably, Johnson inherited the situation from at least three previous administrations. In 1950 President Truman had pledged American "economic and military equipment to the Associated States of Indochina and to France in order to assist them in restoring stability and permitting these states to pursue their peaceful and democratic development." In 1954, after rebels had defeated the French at Dienbienphu, a nineteen-nation conference at Geneva divided French Indochina into Cambodia, Laos, South Vietnam, and Communist-controlled North Vietnam. The Eisenhower administration, while not officially a signatory of the Geneva Accords, issued a unilateral

attempt to bridge a Democratic schism there. As White House cultural affairs gave way to the Johnsons' barbecues on the banks of the Pedernales River, critics concerned more with style than with achievement belittled the President. On at least one occasion, L. B. J. audibly bridled at his critics' reverence for J. F. K. "They say Jack Kennedy had style," he said, "but I'm the one who got the bills passed."

In his conduct of foreign policy, too, Johnson suffered by comparison with Kennedy's graceful image. In an effort to win the confidence of the world's leaders, Johnson addressed the United Nations less than a month after his accession to the Presidency.

statement supporting them, thus endorsing the conference's call for the eventual unification of Vietnam through free elections and an interdict on foreign military intervention there. Eisenhower made a more specific commitment to South Vietnam's Premier Ngo Dinh Diem in a 1954 letter pledging to "assist the government of [South] Vietnam in developing and maintaining a strong viable state, capable of resisting attempted subversion, or aggression through military means," adding the condition that Saigon make every effort to instigate "needed reforms." When Eisenhower left the Presidency, fewer than one thousand American advisers were present in South Vietnam aiding in the fight against Vietcong guerrillas.

Under the Kennedy administration, the United States commitment to South Vietnam in military advisers and personnel rose to twenty-five thousand. This increase induced a counterescalation of opposition forces and of the activities of the National Liberation Front—the Vietcong's political arm—which had been founded in 1960. By September 3, 1963, Kennedy had concluded that Diem was "out of touch with the people" and warned: "In the final analysis, it is their war. We can help them, we can give them equipment, we can send our men out there as advisers but they have to win it."

Facing extreme demands from both left and right in the initial months of his own administration, President Johnson maintained, as late as February, 1964, that the Vietnam War was "first and foremost a contest to be won by the government and the people of that country for themselves." In August, 1964, however, when North Vietnamese torpedo boats twice fired on United States destroyers cruising eleven miles offshore in the Gulf of Tonkin, Johnson ordered retaliatory strikes on North Vietnamese installations. On August 5 he sought and received from Congress a resolution authorizing the President "to take all necessary measures to repel any armed attack against the forces of the United States and to prevent further aggression." The Congress stipulated, however, that all action in this connection must

HUBERT H. HUMPHREY

Lyndon Johnson, according to Senator Russell Long, once called Hubert Horatio Humphrey "the greatest coordinator of mind and tongue in the world, being able to prepare a speech in the time it took to draw a deep breath." Humphrey had other, more practical talents as well, and they resulted in his election to the Vice Presidency in 1964. Johnson, as a senator, had found Humphrey not "like the other liberals. He wanted to get the job done." Politics, to both men, involved hard bargaining and compromise. Born in South Dakota in 1911, Humphrey, a druggist's son, had studied at the University of Minnesota and had then attended the Denver School of Pharmacy so that he could help his family during the Depression. He returned to the university to graduate and then earned his master's degree at Louisiana State in 1940. After working in government and as a teacher, he was elected mayor of Minneapolis in 1945 and senator in 1948, 1954, and 1960. He and Johnson, both of whom were former teachers, New Dealers, and eventually presidential aspirants, became close friends and allies in the Senate. As Vice President he supported Johnson's policies, carried out diplomatic and political missions, and managed the administration's legislative efforts. When L. B. J. decided not to run again in 1968 he threw his support to Humphrey, who therefore became the frontrunner for the nomination.

be consonant with the Constitution of the United States, the Charter of the United Nations, and the SEATO Treaty.

In the presidential campaign of 1964, President Johnson rejected escalation of the war. Facing Arizona's conservative Barry Goldwater, who had been embraced by America's radical right, he said that Goldwater's inflexibility and belief in simplistic military solutions would plunge the nation into nuclear holocaust and that his domestic program would abolish such commonly accepted benefits as Social Security. In city after city, Johnson deplored Goldwater's candid intention to escalate the war in Vietnam toward all-out victory. Repeatedly Johnson assured Americans: "We don't want our American boys to do the fighting for Asian boys. We don't want to get involved in a nation [China] with 700,000,000 people and get tied down in a land war in Asia." Johnson and his liberal running mate, Hubert Humphrey, won the election by the largest popular margin in American history, 43,129,484 votes to 27,178,188.

In accepting the Democratic nomination, Johnson had said: "This nation, this generation, in this hour has man's first chance to build a great society, a place where the meaning of man's life matches the marvel of man's labor." In January, 1965, he pledged new aid to education and to urban renewal, a war on disease and on air and water pollution, aid to depressed areas, and an end to voting restrictions based on color.

Again Johnson's leadership of Congress was phenomenal. Outstanding among his administration's achievements were laws authorizing unprecedented, massive federal aid to elementary and secondary schools; Medicare, which provided medical aid to those over sixty-five through the Social Security system; federal aid to the deprived Appalachian states; liberalized immigration; housing; and the creation of a Department of Housing and Urban Development. Under Johnson, too, America recovered its position in the space race, matching, in the summer of 1965, Russia's famed walk in space. And under Johnson the states ratified the Twenty-fifth Amendment, which provided for an orderly transfer of presidential power in the event of presidential incapacitation, resignation, or removal from office, and granted the President the power to name— with the approval of Congress—a new Vice President in the event of a vacancy.

The President's supreme achievement was the passage of the Voting Rights Act of 1965. In a dramatic nighttime personal appearance before Congress, Johnson urged passage of a law authorizing federal voting registrars to assure electoral justice to Negroes in areas where they were denied the vote. The Negroes' cause, he declared, "must be our cause too. Because it's not just Negroes, but really it's all of us who must overcome the crippling legacy of bigotry and injustice." Then Johnson gave presidential voice to the hymn of civil rights marchers: "And," said the President, "we shall overcome."

Another Caribbean crisis erupted in April, 1965, when a revolt broke out in the Dominican Republic. The President sent some

In this 1967 cartoon, the Democratic donkey watches in consternation as President Johnson tries to keep astride the widening "Credibility Gap."

Johnson conferred in August, 1966, with General William Westmoreland, commander in Vietnam.

twenty thousand troops to restore order. He subsequently justified this extreme action by insisting that "we don't propose to sit here in our rocking chair with our hands folded and let the Communists set up any government in the Western Hemisphere." But Communist involvement was questionable, and Johnson's response to the uprising badly damaged United States prestige.

In other major areas, however, Johnson's approach was marked by admirable restraint. Consistently nettled by France's Charles de Gaulle, who ordered NATO out of France in early 1967, Johnson maintained a dignified silence. Denounced by Peking, he refused to return invective. With the Soviet Union he continued to maintain *détente*, sustaining cultural exchange, urging the cooperative exploration of outer space, and signing in 1967 a historic treaty increasing the number of consulates in both nations.

The war in Vietnam, however, continued to escalate. On February 7, 1965, when Vietcong terrorists attacked an American military installation at Pleiku, Johnson ordered air strikes on North Vietnam that, as time passed, increased in intensity. On April 7, 1965, speaking in Baltimore, the President made United States policy explicit: "The central lesson of our time," he de-

clared, "is that the appetite of aggression is never satisfied. . . . We must say in Southeast Asia, as we did in Europe, in the words of the Bible: 'Hitherto shalt thou come; but no further.' . . . Our objective is the independence of South Vietnam and its freedom from attack. . . . We will not withdraw, either openly or under the cloak of a meaningless agreement."

By November, 1965, the United States had committed 165,700 troops to Vietnam. Whereas 146 Americans were killed in battle in 1964, 1,104 died in 1965. In 1966, 5,008 Americans were killed and 30,093 wounded. Early in 1967, American artillery fired over the demilitarized zone into North Vietnam, the United States Navy bombarded the North Vietnamese shore, and the United States Air Force dropped mines into North Vietnamese rivers.

In March, Johnson met at Guam with South Vietnam's Premier, Nguyen Cao Ky (Ngo Dinh Diem had been overthrown in 1963), and with General William C. Westmoreland, commander of United States troops in Vietnam, in talks widely believed to foreshadow further escalation of the war. The President announced his determination "to resist aggression, and to make possible the sacred work of peace among men." By late April, United States planes had bombed Haiphong Harbor, Haiphong itself, and MIG fighter plane bases in the North. On April 26, United States jets struck at Hanoi's bridged rail link with China.

The bombing of the MIG airfields evoked new protests from prominent critics of the war. And when General Westmoreland, summoned to the United States by Johnson, declared that peace protests were encouraging Hanoi to continue its aggression, the administration was accused of attempting to stifle dissent and criticism at home.

Democrat George McGovern rose in the Senate to condemn the bombings as bringing the nation "one step closer to World War III involving the limitless legions of China backed by the enormous firepower of Soviet Russia. So I do not intend to remain silent in the face of what I regard as a policy of madness. . . ." Joined by Senators Robert Kennedy, J. William Fulbright, Frank Church, and Ernest Gruening, he charged that the Johnson administration was "confessing the weakness of its own case by trying to silence its critics. . . ." Quoting the Roman general Tacitus, Kennedy added: "We made a desert and we called it peace."

The liberal senators, sixteen of whom later issued a statement saying that although they urged negotiations, they did not advocate unilateral withdrawal of American troops, were not alone in their criticism of the administration's conduct of the war and its commitment of some 460,000 American troops by May 1, 1967. Many distinguished clergymen, professors, lawyers, and intellectual leaders joined the swelling ranks of unimpeachably loyal Americans who marched in protest against the war.

"The nation," Walter Lippmann warned, "is being governed without the support of, against the feeling of, great segments of its spiritual and intellectual leadership." Republican Senator Charles Percy declared that the administration's insistence that negotiations exclude the Vietcong was "unrealistic." Percy said, "We must answer whether we are prepared to allow our men to die at the rate of 150 to 250 a month, for an interminable number of years, in search of a total victory which cannot, in my judgment, really be achieved." Mississippi's Senator John Stennis, on the other hand, wanted to "remove the arbitrary restrictions and widen and expand the air war so as to strike all militarily significant targets. . . ." Others complained that the administration had not gone far enough and urged the bombing of Hanoi or war with China itself.

On May 19, American planes bombarded downtown Hanoi for the first time. Later that month, a new record for one week's American casualties was set: 2,929. And by July 2, the total number of United States troops killed in Vietnam stood at 11,323, with 68,341 wounded and 674 missing.

With the eruption of war in the Mideast in June, 1967, the administration faced a new challenge. Egyptian President Nasser's blockade of the Gulf of Aqaba (site of the strategic Israeli port of Elath) and the build-up of Arab forces along Israel's borders culminated in a massive Israeli offensive. Within six days, Israeli forces had thrust through the Sinai Peninsula to Suez, cleared the gulf, and seized Old Jerusalem and parts of Jordan and Syria. Israel's stunning victory was challenged by the Soviet Union, major supplier of arms to the Arabs. Premier Aleksei Kosygin himself flew to New York to demand—without success—that the United Nations condemn Israel.

Johnson maintained a studied neutrality in the crisis. Refusing to intervene in the fighting, L. B. J. declined to participate in the acrimonious debates at the United Nations, where Ambassador Arthur Goldberg urged direct Arab-Israeli negotiations with the aid of a third party. From Washington, Johnson called on the belligerents to honor "the recognized right of national life" and urged "justice for refugees . . . innocent maritime passage . . . limits on the . . . arms race . . . [and] political independence and territorial integrity for all." A historic Summit Conference, held by Johnson and Kosygin in Glassboro, New Jersey, produced no substantive results, both sides remaining adamant in their positions on Vietnam and the Mideast. But Johnson emerged from the talks with renewed stature, with an image of statesmanlike restraint. Most Americans agreed with the President that although amiable conversation does not in itself produce peace, "it does help a lot to sit down and look at a man right in the eye and try to reason with him. . . ."

Civil rights advocates were delighted in June by Johnson's appointment of Thurgood Marshall, a Negro, to the Supreme Court. Optimism gave way to despair in July, however, when massive Negro rioting in major American cities led to intervention by federal troops. "Looting, and arson, and plunder, and pillage," Johnson declared, "are not part of a civil rights protest. . . . And crime must be dealt with forcefully, and certainly, under law." Johnson's critics, however, charged that the President

Senator Eugene McCarthy announces that he will enter several presidential primaries in 1968.

himself had to share much of the blame for the riots, since the huge cost of the Vietnam War had forced drastic cutbacks in programs to relieve the urban poor and to fight racial bias in housing and employment.

In this climate of protest the United States was more sharply divided than at any time since the closing months of the Truman administration. By early autumn, 1967, L. B. J.'s government by "consensus" had split at the seams. In late September fifty-two House members cited a "growing uneasiness in Congress" over the "Americanization" of the Vietnam War despite Congress' limitation (in the Tonkin Resolution) of the American role to one of assistance. Senator Clifford Case of New Jersey, a moderate Republican, decried a "crisis of confidence" provoked by Johnson's alleged misuse of the resolution. Republican Senator Thruston Morton of Kentucky admitted that he had been wrong in supporting Johnson on Vietnam, and charged that the President had been brainwashed by the "military-industrial complex" into pushing for total victory. Democratic Senators Wayne Morse and J. William Fulbright, who maintained incessant fire on their party chief, were joined

more vigorously by Robert F. Kennedy, who charged that Johnson had "switched" from J. F. K.'s moderate Vietnam policy, thereby gravely weakening the nation's moral position.

The most startling Democratic challenge to Johnson occurred on November 30, when liberal Senator Eugene McCarthy of Minnesota announced that he would enter the 1968 presidential primaries, and would campaign chiefly on the issue of Vietnam. "My decision to challenge the President's position," McCarthy said, "has been strengthened by recent announcements from the Administration of plans for continued escalation and intensification of the war in Vietnam and, on the other hand, by the absence of any positive indications or suggestions for a compromise or negotiated political settlement. I am concerned that the Administration seems to have set no limits on the price that it will pay for military victory."

In Congress Johnson suffered major setbacks. Republican senators generally backed his programs, but recalcitrant House Republicans and Dixiecrats slashed the administration's antipoverty, open housing, crime control, model cities, and foreign aid programs. A 10 per cent surtax on income—which Johnson regarded as imperative—was not even reported out of committee.

It was L. B. J.'s darkest hour in the White House. Even his staunch Republican ally, Senate Minority Leader Everett Dirksen, spoke out against him at the end of the year. "As our casualties mount daily . . ." Dirksen said, "the unpopularity of the war among our people intensifies hourly and there is little evident reason to hope for victory in the foreseeable future. For there is no prospect of peace, no promise of stability, no hope for the better in the policies of this Administration." Nor could Johnson take comfort from a massive peace march to the Pentagon in late October, during which potential violence was checked only by the presence of armed federal troops and marshals. Campus demonstrations, picketing of draft induction centers, and ritual burning of draft cards occurred in various parts of the nation. Several prominent retired military leaders attacked the war as militarily and morally unsound.

Politically, Johnson appeared to be in trouble. Pollster George Gallup said that the 1968 presidential contest might be the hardest to predict since 1948. Polls indicated that although Johnson might defeat Richard M. Nixon, he would be trounced by Nelson Rockefeller of New York.

L. B. J., however, did not seem to be alarmed by these portents of defeat. He had a poll of his own to cite: Gallup's year-end finding that 46 per cent of America's adults approved his handling of the Presidency, as opposed to 38 per cent the previous October. Addressing the AFL-CIO convention in early December, Johnson came out fighting, blasting the G.O.P. congressmen who had crippled his Great Society reforms: "In vote after vote," he declared, House Republicans had "lined up like wooden soldiers of the status quo," voting to kill Medicare, antipoverty funds, housing and rent supplements, and the minimum wage bill. "But they are not fooling anybody," Johnson cried, "are they? The people know that the old Republican buggy can go only one way —and that's backwards, downhill. . . ." Having triumphantly signed the Wholesome Meat and Flammable Fabrics acts—which extended federal supervision to those industries—the President enplaned on a 27,600-mile Christmas tour. At Camranh Bay in Vietnam, he assured servicemen that North Vietnam could not win. Home again, L. B. J. signed a law granting at least a 13 per cent increase in Social Security payments to twenty-four million Americans.

Late in January, 1968, the Vietcong attacked six major South Vietnamese cities with unprecedented force, assaulting even the American embassy in Saigon. In twelve days of fighting, 973 Americans, 2,119 South Vietnamese, and an estimated 30,795 enemy soldiers were killed. The administration was assailed for underestimating enemy strength and will and for overestimating the prospects for an Allied victory. Nor did the seizure of the American intelligence ship *Pueblo* by North Korea bolster American pride or

Johnson's prestige. In March, Senator McCarthy won a stunning 42.4 per cent of the vote and twenty of the twenty-four delegates in New Hampshire's Democratic primary. McCarthy's showing prompted Senator Robert F. Kennedy to challenge L. B. J. for the nomination. Kennedy swiftly took to the campaign trail, condemning the President's war policy as "bankrupt."

But L. B. J. had a surprise of his own. On March 31, in one of the most dramatic political moves in American history, Johnson shocked the world by announcing that he would neither seek nor accept his party's nomination in 1968. ". . . I have concluded," he said, "that I should not permit the Presidency to become involved in the partisan divisions. . . ." He also announced the suspension of bombing over 76 per cent of North Vietnam and again invited Hanoi to the peace table.

Peace talks began in Paris in May, but dragged on for months without results. The war remained a major issue in the presidential primaries, in which Senators McCarthy and Kennedy together overwhelmed slates associated with Vice President Humphrey, the President's clear choice. Then, in June, politics gave way to grief when Kennedy was assassinated in California. It was the second such tragedy to strike the nation within three months; in April, Martin Luther King, Jr., the apostle of nonviolence, had been killed in Memphis. After Kennedy's death, the President appointed a commission to investigate why violence was so prevalent in American life.

During the summer, L. B. J. flew to Central America to discuss an aid program and to Honolulu to meet with South Vietnamese officials. By agreeing to budget cuts, he finally won his income tax surcharge from Congress. He locked horns with Senate conservatives over the appointment of Abe Fortas as Chief Justice and with the steel industry over price increases. Although a self-proclaimed lame duck President, Lyndon Johnson remained as active, as determined, and as unpredictable as ever.

—WILSON SULLIVAN

[signature: Lyndon B. Johnson]

A PICTURE PORTFOLIO

The Western background of Lyndon Baines Johnson was emphasized by the 1964 campaign item above. This ten-gallon hat was reproduced to be worn on Democratic lapels.

"LYNDON IS
UNRELENTING, TOO"

Lyndon and Lady Bird Johnson, who were married on November 17, 1934, were photographed near Mexico City during their honeymoon trip (above).

It was a hard land from which Lyndon B. Johnson came. His wife called it "unrelenting country," adding, "Lyndon is unrelenting, too." From the day in 1932 when—just out of teachers college and a job in a Houston high school—he came to Washington as secretary to Representative Richard M. Kleberg, he demonstrated his drive. By 1937 he had been elected to the House of Representatives; in 1948 he was chosen senator. Johnson understood power, and understanding it, was drawn to it. Power begins at home in politics. Thus he followed President Roosevelt's New Deal in response to the needs and wishes of his home district but later shifted to the right to accommodate the larger constituency of his home state as a whole—particularly the petroleum interests whose money was becoming a key to Texas elections. Power in Washington depends less on what a man believes than on how he goes about his business. As representative and senator, Johnson carefully cultivated his peers and superiors, particularly Roosevelt, congressional old hands such as Sam Rayburn and Georgia's Senator Richard Russell, and influential New Dealers—the people who made things tick in the Capital. His love of politics—he talked about it all the time— and his avoidance of doctrinaire attitudes on issues endeared him to the professionals. Most important, although Johnson remained sufficiently conservative to satisfy Texas and the powers that were in Congress, he tried to walk a path near the middle of American political philosophy; national power depended on his enlarging his constituency to national size—something no major Southern figure since Andrew Jackson, "the People's President," had been able to do. Lyndon Baines Johnson's reward was his election in 1953—when he was only forty-four years old—to the important post of Senate Minority Leader.

Above, Johnson meets President Roosevelt at Galveston, Texas, in 1937 after winning, on a strongly pro-New Deal platform, a special election for a seat in Congress. Below, the young Texan campaigns for the Senate in 1941, a race he barely lost. Behind him are his wife, left, and his mother, Rebekah Baines Johnson.

Above, Lyndon Johnson, the Senate Majority Leader, attends a 1958 Memorial Day ceremony at Franklin Roosevelt's grave. Mrs. Roosevelt, left, supported Stevenson rather than Johnson or Kennedy in 1960.

After losing the Democratic convention battle to Kennedy, Johnson surprised everyone, including J. F. K., by accepting second place on the 1960 ticket. Above, with his wife beside him, he salutes the cheering delegates.

CZAR OF THE SENATE

If the Senate leadership could be concentrated instead of broken up into sectional groups, Lyndon Johnson realized, the Upper House could wield much more power in the federal government. As Minority Leader during the first two years of the Eisenhower administration and Majority Leader from 1955 to 1960, Johnson was not only leader of the Senate Democrats in voting and in debate; because of the many friendships and alliances he had built and because his position made him chairman of three major Democratic caucus committees, he was master of the machinery that could make him a virtual czar of the Senate. With the acquiescence of the long-time *de facto* boss of the conservative Senate Democrats, Richard Russell—with whom Johnson had a good, carefully nurtured working relationship—he broke the traditional seniority rule for committee appointments. He could therefore name newer senators to important committees, which brought double dividends: the senators who had been placed in prestigious posts were grateful and repaid him in votes; and by spreading around the major assignments he cut the power of the seniority-heavy conservatives and increased his own power correspondingly. Such weapons as the handing out of Senate campaign funds and of choice office space were also used to build a united Johnsonian Senate. The results were often spectacular. "Lyndon's passed bills in a few days that I thought would take weeks," said the Senate parliamentarian, Charles Watkins. Among those bills were the first two civil rights acts in nearly a century. He was Majority Leader in a larger than usual sense: he acted as the chief embodiment of the national pro-Eisenhower consensus and helped pass Ike's legislation—sometimes in the face of Republican opposition. He thus became widely known and respected, a strong presidential possibility, and, in 1961, John Fitzgerald Kennedy's Vice President.

After years of great power and prominence, Johnson settled uneasily into the relative limbo of the Vice Presidency (above). "Lyndon's job," the President said, "is the hardest one he could ever have—and he is performing it like a man, M-A-N."

In the cabin of the presidential airplane, Air Force One, *ninety-eight minutes after John Kennedy was declared dead, Lyndon Johnson was sworn in as President (above) by United States District Judge Sarah Hughes. He is flanked by Lady Bird Johnson and Mrs. John F. Kennedy.*

Two days after the assassination, the alleged killer, *Lee Harvey Oswald, was himself murdered (below) by Dallas night-club operator Jack Ruby while police stood by helplessly and millions of Americans watched on television. This, among other weird aspects of the assassination and its aftermath, raised fears that Oswald, if he was indeed the murderer, had acted as part of a conspiracy.*

CECIL B. STOUGHTON

© 1963 BOB JACKSON, THE DALLAS *Times Herald*

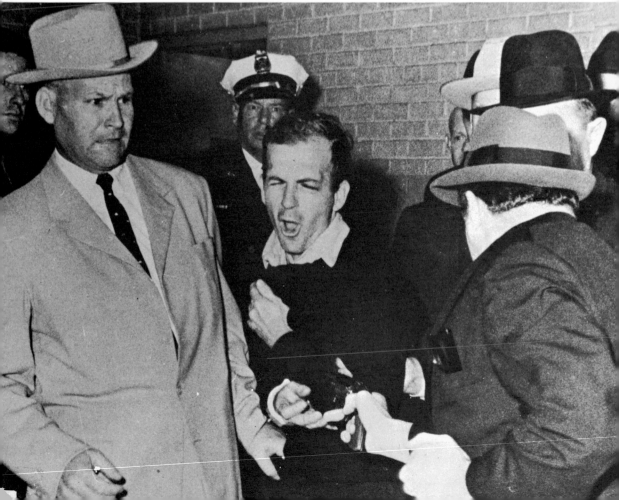

TRANSITION

Lyndon Johnson, a man with an intense need to act forcefully, had been dutifully hobbling himself for a thousand days, and could look forward to two thousand more of the same. Suddenly, because of an incredible tragedy, action was demanded of him. For the eighth time in one hundred and seventy-four years, a Vice President acceded to the powers of a deceased Chief Executive. Ominously, the assassination had taken place in Johnson's state, during a fence-mending visit demanded by a local party feud between liberals and conservatives for which Johnson had been partly responsible and for which he had been unable to provide a remedy. For the first time since the threatening cold war began, an emergency transition of power had to be effected; the dead President had been better loved around the world than any predecessor, except possibly Franklin Roosevelt, and his place was to be taken by a man believed to be more a politician than a statesman, a man who was not so beloved nor so well-known. In the midst of national sorrow, Johnson took charge quickly. He set up a commission to investigate the assassination; he smoothed the transition and proved his faithfulness to the Kennedy tradition by asking Congress for—and getting—quick action on New Frontier legislation. Some of those closest to Kennedy could not forgive Johnson for taking over the Presidency with such sureness. But most Americans were grateful that John F. Kennedy had chosen so well at Los Angeles in 1960.

As the photograph above illustrates, the official report on the assassination, issued by the special commission headed by Chief Justice Earl Warren, did not end public questioning about the dismaying events in Dallas.

The new President addressed Congress on November 27, 1963 (top right). World leaders looked on anxiously—as the London Daily Express cartoon above indicates. Johnson was identified with Texas, which was considered by foreigners to be strange country even before John Kennedy was killed there.

BOTH: WIDE WORLD

"AN ELEMENTAL FORCE"

Because the Eastern liberals distrusted Lyndon Johnson the Texas politician (in much the same way that rural Protestants had distrusted Kennedy the Catholic), it was often said that only through the Vice Presidency and succession by death could he have reached the White House. Being a sensitive man who was proud of his contribution to government, Johnson resented that deeply. Therefore it was inevitable that he would attempt to demonstrate that he deserved to be Chief Executive every bit as much as his predecessor had. In the process he created his own version of the Presidency. Kennedy had been rather gentle with Congress; Johnson brought it to heel as he forced it to approve the sale of wheat to Russia and to pass a strong civil rights act, federal aid to mass transportation and to education, and the antipoverty bill—all within nine months of the assassination. He used the telephone frequently to urge individual congressmen to back legislation. He made it clear that *he* was to make important decisions, not his advisers—among whom he labored to produce consensus support for whatever he wanted to do. In foreign affairs, as at home, he tried to operate on an intense face-to-face basis. When the republic of Panama cut diplomatic ties with the United States in January, 1964, he broke all the rules and placed a long-distance call to the Panamanian president. "LBJ has been hurling himself about Washington like an elemental force," commented *The New Republic*. "To be plain about it, he has won our admiration. . . ."

At left, in Panama, National Guardsmen break up one of the anti-American demonstrations over the Canal Zone that disrupted relations between the two nations for much of 1964. The central issue was renegotiation of the Canal treaty. Domestic politics made the presidents of each of the involved countries leery of seeming to give in to the other, but by that April a review of the old treaty had commenced.

BARRY M. GOLDWATER

"In your heart you know he's right," said Barry Goldwater's supporters during the election of 1964. The opinion of most Americans, however, was summed up in a pun: Goldwater was too *far* right. A native of Phoenix, Arizona, Goldwater had attended military schools and the University of Arizona, and then had taken a job in the family business, a department store. A member of the Arizona National Guard, he was assigned to the Air Force in 1941 and served as a pilot and instructor during World War II. Named to the Phoenix city council in 1949, when he was forty years old, Goldwater was elected to the United States Senate three years later. There he displayed the stern conservatism and anti-Communist militancy that made him the hero of the American right. The conservatives, believing that the Republican party should offer the electorate "a choice, not an echo," gained control of crucial state organizations and thus of the 1964 national convention and nominated Goldwater for President. But most voters were appalled by his alleged readiness to use nuclear weapons freely in war, by the extremism of some of his partisans, and by his seemingly outdated view of the role of government. They were not swayed by his personal attractiveness and gave him only fifty-two electoral votes. He retired to private life following his defeat, but Goldwater's admirers urged him to run for the United States Senate again in 1968.

A SMASHING VICTORY

Since the Civil War, no candidate from a state that had joined the Confederacy had been elected President. But in 1964 that tradition was broken—appropriately enough, by Johnson, master of domestic consensus and moderation. Because he had committed himself to a New Deal type of program—the Great Society—he had become attractive to the urban centers of the Northeast, where he had only recently been believed to be weakest. So, even before the conservative Republicans nominated Senator Goldwater and deliberately alienated the moderates in their party, it appeared that Johnson would win the election. Goldwater's nomination gave the President an opportunity not just to win but to win big, which he longed to do in order to move out from under the shadow of his succession by death. Yet despite the sense of triumph that surrounded him through the autumn, it was reported that this complicated man sometimes brooded over the inescapable fact that many pro-Johnson votes would stem not from admiration for him, but from antipathy to Goldwater. Nevertheless, his campaign consciously encouraged such "anti" votes. It was clear when the returns were in that Johnson had left behind much of the Deep South in his move toward the middle: the electoral votes of five Southern states went to Goldwater. But President Johnson won a record share of the nationwide popular vote: 61 per cent.

Lyndon Johnson and Hubert H. Humphrey—two farm-land populists, long-time allies, and, by L. B. J.'s 1964 decision, running mates—confer aboard the presidential jet (above) en route to the Democratic convention in Atlantic City, New Jersey. Johnson is watching his own nomination on television.

Johnson's campaign caught fire in New England late in September. From then on his crowds were huge and enthusiastic, his momentum was uncheck-able. Below, he is greeted in Tennessee two weeks before the voting.

CONSENSUS AND
THE GREAT SOCIETY

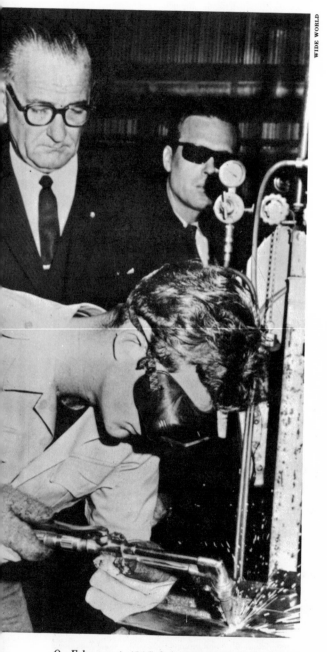

On February 1, 1965, five months after Congress set up the Job Corps to train underprivileged youngsters, the first center was opened in Oregon. Above, Johnson visits a center in Texas later that year.

The Great Society was no mirage, no political ploy to be used in a campaign and then allowed to dwindle away. The legislative achievements of Johnson's first three months in office after his 1965 inauguration amply justified his claim of "a record of major accomplishments without equal or close parallel in the present era." They included passage of a plan for medical care for the aged (within the Social Security system), federal aid to elementary and secondary education, and aid to the impoverished areas in the Appalachians. "Indeed," wrote journalists Rowland Evans and Robert Novak, "Johnson kept one eye on the calendar in his frantic exhortations to the congressional leaders to pass as many bills as possible during *his* Hundred Days . . . ." L. B. J. did not slow down after his triumphs: later in 1965, Congress was prodded into passing a voting rights act to ensure political rights of Negroes; it also loosened immigration restrictions, created the Department of Housing and Urban Development, and set up the Economic Development Administration. "Toscanini was a great conductor, right?" one Johnson aide said. "He knew what the second violin could do, what the brass could do, what the whole orchestra could do. That's like Lyndon. . . . He's a political artist of genius." But columnist Max Lerner lamented "the smell of power that pervades L. B. J. and everything associated with him," and James Reston of *The New York Times* noted that Johnson "would like to call all the signals, carry the ball on every play and run his own interference." A member of Johnson's staff said, "He's liable to wake up in the morning and think everything's got loose in the night." And when, as was bound to happen, the national consensus that Johnson was so proud of began to crack, he responded to opposition as if it were a personal affront.

Above, retired workers demanding passage of Medicare picket a meeting of the American Medical Association.

Below is a rural North Carolina family—living in the kind of poverty that Johnson hoped to eliminate.

REBELLIONS

Johnson's legislative record was among the most remarkable in United States history; and astronaut Edward White's walk in space, the progress of the war on poverty, and the national beautification program (in which the President's competent wife took an active interest) filled him with pride of accomplishment. But in 1965, as the Great Society was propelled thunderously onward, the President had his troubles. Despite his continuing efforts for civil rights, Negroes were more and more impatient: there were marches, riots, and demonstrations. And the liberals, who had been backing him because of his domestic program, began sniping at his foreign policy in April, when the President, fearing that a civil war in the Dominican Republic would lead to a Communist take-over there, ordered United States Marines into the Caribbean republic. Johnson was upset by the attacks and tried desperately to win back liberal support. But many of his critics were implacable. In his book *Lyndon B. Johnson and the World*, Philip Geyelin wrote that Johnson's "irrelevant rationalizations and often inaccurate reconstruction of events [had changed] an essentially unmanageable and, in some ways, unavoidable crisis . . . into a crisis of confidence in [him]."

"It's fun. I'm not coming in," said an exhila-rated Edward White as ground control tried to get him to end his walk in space (top, left)—high-light of a record-setting two-man mission in 1965.

Above, American paratroopers watch over Santo Domingo during the Dominican Republic crisis.

Thirty-five people died, and hundreds were hurt, in a race riot (left) in the Watts area of Los Angeles.

1057

NAMES IN THE NEWS

ALL: WIDE WORLD

DEAN RUSK

While noting Dean Rusk's "exceptional intelligence, lucidity and control" and his "talent for concise and dispassionate exposition," Arthur Schlesinger, Jr., described the Secretary of State as "irrevocably conventional." But if John Kennedy, who appointed Rusk to his Cabinet in 1961, found him exasperating at times (he "never gives me anything to chew on. . . . You never know what he is thinking"), Lyndon Johnson regarded him as a "wise counselor." "He is Number One in the Cabinet and he is Number One with me," Johnson said. Rusk once wrote that he agreed with Harry Truman's dictum "The President makes foreign policy." He served Johnson as a loyal chief of staff and administration spokesman, especially for Johnson's policies in Vietnam. The son of a tenant farmer, the Georgia-born Rusk had attended Davidson College and had been a Rhodes scholar at Oxford; later he was dean of faculty at Mills College in California. He served in Asia during World War II, after which he held several posts in the State Department. In 1951 he was named president of the Rockefeller Foundation. A firm, patient negotiator, he became a seemingly imperturbable Secretary of State. "We're eyeball to eyeball," he said during the Cuban Missile Crisis, "and I think the other fellow just blinked."

MARTIN LUTHER KING, JR.

"He has an indescribable capacity for empathy that is the touchstone of leadership," wrote *Time* magazine of the Reverend Dr. Martin Luther King, Jr. A Baptist clergyman and a doctor of theology, King emerged as a leader in the civil rights movement in 1955 while he was serving as a pastor in Montgomery, Alabama. Spurred into action by a bus segregation incident, he accepted the leadership of the Montgomery Improvement Association and directed a yearlong Negro boycott of city buses. His first major civil rights victory occurred in 1956 when the Supreme Court declared the Alabama bus segregation laws unconstitutional. An advocate of nonviolent resistance, Dr. King led subsequent protests throughout the United States, using civil disobedience as a weapon against discriminatory laws. "From my Christian background I gained my ideals," he once said, "and from Gandhi my operational technique." In 1963 King helped to organize a massive march on Washington, D.C., by citizens—whites as well as Negroes—who demanded the passage of a civil rights bill; the following year he was awarded the Nobel Peace Prize. In 1967 he urged immediate de-escalation of the Vietnam War. Dr. King was assassinated on April 4, 1968, in Memphis, Tennessee, where he had gone to support striking sanitation workers.

J. WILLIAM FULBRIGHT

"The most striking characteristic of a great nation," said Senator J. William Fulbright in 1965, "is ... the wisdom and restraint ... with which power is exercised." Chairman of the Committee on Foreign Relations since 1959, Senator Fulbright stated that the United States had, in Southeast Asia, revealed an "arrogance of power"; he also felt that the nation tended, as in the case of President Johnson's intervention in the Dominican Republic, to make "exaggerated estimates of Communist influence." These views made Fulbright a leader of those opposed to administration policy in Vietnam. He maintained that the cost of a complete military victory there would far exceed "the requirements of our interest and our honor," and urged a "negotiated settlement involving major concessions by both sides." Fulbright, a 1925 graduate of the University of Arkansas, was later a Rhodes scholar at Oxford and a law student at George Washington University. He then taught law and became president of the University of Arkansas in 1939. Elected to the House of Representatives on the Democratic ticket in 1942, he was sent to the Senate in 1944. Author of a resolution that led to the organization of the United Nations, Senator Fulbright sponsored a 1946 act establishing scholarships for American and foreign exchange students.

THURGOOD MARSHALL

Thurgood Marshall built a remarkable legal career on his conviction that all forms of racial segregation were unconstitutional. Born in Baltimore in 1908, he was educated in segregated schools. After his graduation from Howard University Law School in 1933, he established a practice and specialized in civil rights cases. In his capacity as special counsel to the National Association for the Advancement of Colored People, Marshall led the assault on state segregation laws, especially in the field of education. He argued thirty-two cases before the United States Supreme Court and won all but three of them. As a result of his efforts, Virginia's law ordering segregated seating in buses was declared to be unconstitutional when interstate travel was involved, and Texas Negroes were guaranteed the right to vote in primaries and serve on juries. His most dramatic success occurred in 1954, when the Court ruled that separate educational facilities were inherently unequal, and that segregated schools were therefore unconstitutional. In 1961 Marshall was appointed by President John F. Kennedy to the United States Court of Appeals. He was named Solicitor General five years later, and served in that post until 1967, when Lyndon B. Johnson selected Marshall to become the first Negro justice of the Supreme Court.

"RESTLESSNESS"

As Johnson's second term progressed, the war in Vietnam became the center of national attention and of bitter controversy. Johnson's policy was two-pronged: he selectively increased the military pressure on the North Vietnamese while at the same time hunting for diplomatic solutions. But as the death toll of American soldiers in Vietnam rose steadily, as reports of corruption in the South Vietnamese government were publicized, and as escalation of the American effort increased fears of Red Chinese intervention, President Johnson was caught in a cross fire from his critics, some of whom wanted more fighting, and some, less.

In his 1968 State of the Union message, Johnson observed that there was "in the land a certain restlessness, a questioning." It seemed to political observers that the

In the photograph at left, residents of Hanoi wait in bomb shelters for the all-clear siren. At center, antiwar demonstrators gather in New York's Central Park before a "peace march" to the United Nations in 1967.

1968 election would indicate to what degree Americans held Johnson responsible for their disquiet. The substantial vote accorded Senator Eugene McCarthy in the New Hampshire primary early in March, and the subsequent support for Senator Robert Kennedy's candidacy, indicated dramatically how divided the country was over Johnson's policies. Then, on March 31, the President appeared on television to announce both a pause in the bombing of most of North Vietnam and his decision not to seek re-election. "But let men everywhere know, however," Johnson concluded firmly, "that a strong and a confident and a vigilant America stands ready tonight to seek an honorable peace; and stands ready tonight to defend an honorable cause, whatever the price, whatever the burden, whatever the sacrifice that duty may require."

American soldiers of the 1st Cavalry Division climb up to a hovering helicopter in South Vietnam, above. Troops from Australia, New Zealand, and South Korea also aided the South Vietnamese in their fight.

FACTS IN SUMMARY: LYNDON BAINES JOHNSON

CHRONOLOGY

UNITED STATES		JOHNSON
Taft elected President	1908	Born August 27
Coolidge elected President	1924	Graduates from high school
	1927	Graduates from Southwest Texas State Teachers College
Stock market crash	1929	
	1930	Begins teaching in Houston
	1931	Campaigns for election of Richard Kleberg to Congress
Roosevelt elected President	1932	Goes to Washington as Kleberg's secretary
New Deal legislation	1933	
NLRB created	1934	Marries Claudia Taylor
Social Security Act	1935	Named director of National Youth Administration in Texas
	1937	Elected to Congress
	1938	Re-elected to Congress
Roosevelt re-elected	1940	Serves as chairman of Democratic Congressional Campaign Committee
		Re-elected to Congress
Pearl Harbor bombed	1941	Loses special U.S. Senate election
U.S. enters World War II		Goes on active duty in Navy
Battle of Midway	1942	Sent to Pacific as President's representative
Battle of Guadalcanal		Awarded Silver Star Medal
Invasion of North Africa		Re-elected to Congress
U.S. offensives in Pacific and Italy	1943	
Allies land in France	1944	Serves on Committee on Postwar Military Policy
Philippines Campaign begins		
Truman becomes President	1945	
Atomic bomb dropped on Hiroshima		
Paris Peace Conference	1946	Re-elected to Congress
Truman Doctrine	1947	Serves on House Armed Services Committee
Marshall Plan		Votes for Taft-Hartley Act
Berlin Airlift	1948	Serves on Joint Committee on Atomic Energy
Truman elected President		Elected to Senate
NATO pact signed	1949	Serves on Senate Armed Services Committee
Russia explodes atomic bomb		

UNITED STATES		JOHNSON
Korean War begins	1950	Heads Senate Preparedness Investigating Subcommittee
	1951	Elected Democratic Whip in Senate
Eisenhower elected President	1952	
Armistice in Korea	1953	Chosen Senate Minority Leader
Supreme Court desegregation order	1954	Re-elected to Senate
Army-McCarthy hearings		Elected Senate Majority Leader
	1955	Suffers heart attack
School integration crisis in Little Rock	1957	Manages passage of Civil Rights Act
First U.S. satellite orbited	1958	Serves as chairman of Special Space and Astronautics Committee
Fidel Castro comes to power in Cuba	1959	Named chairman of Aeronautical and Space Sciences Committee
U-2 shot down in Russia	1960	Loses presidential nomination to Kennedy
Kennedy elected President		Accepts vice presidential nomination
		Elected Vice President
Eisenhower breaks off diplomatic relations with Cuba	1961	Named head of the National Aeronautics and Space Council
Peace Corps created		Appointed chairman of President's Committee on Equal Employment Opportunity
Invasion of Cuba by exiles fails		
Berlin Wall built		Sent to Asia and Berlin by President
Lt. Col. Glenn orbits earth	1962	Makes Middle Eastern trip for Kennedy
Cuban Missile Crisis		Meets OAS ambassadors at LBJ ranch
Limited nuclear test ban treaty signed	1963	Becomes President
Civil rights supporters march on Washington		Appoints Warren Commission to investigate Kennedy assassination
Kennedy assassinated in Dallas		Urges passage of Civil Rights Act
Riots in Panama Canal Zone	1964	Acts to settle controversy with Panama
Twenty-fourth Amendment ratified		Announces war on poverty
Civil Rights Act passed		Forces settlement of railroad strike
North Vietnamese torpedo boats attack U.S. destroyers		Signs Civil Rights Act
		Orders retaliatory bombing of North Vietnam
Congress gives President emergency powers for Vietnam conflict		Signs Economic Opportunity Act
		Elected President

Vietcong attack U.S. installation at Pleiku	1965	*Orders resumption of bombing of North Vietnam*
Dominican Republic crisis		*Sends U.S. troops to end Dominican uprising*
Race riots in Los Angeles		*Signs Medicare Act and Voting Rights Act*
First U.S. "soft" lunar landing	1966	*Meets with Premier Ky in Honolulu*
U.S. bombs Hanoi		*Attends Manila Conference on Vietnam*
Escalation of U.S. bombing of North Vietnam	1967	*Meets with Premier Kosygin at Glassboro*
War in Middle East		*Names Thurgood Marshall to Supreme Court*
Riots in U.S. cities		
North Korea seizes U.S. ship	1968	*Announces pause in bombing of North Vietnam and states that he will not seek re-election*
Martin Luther King assassinated		
Robert F. Kennedy assassinated		*Announces that peace talks will be held in Paris*

BIOGRAPHICAL FACTS

BIRTH: Near Stonewall, Tex., Aug. 27, 1908

ANCESTRY: English

FATHER: Samuel Ealy Johnson, Jr.; b. Buda, Tex., Oct. 11, 1877; d. Austin, Tex., Oct. 11, 1937

FATHER'S OCCUPATIONS: Schoolteacher; farmer; state legislator

MOTHER: Rebekah Baines Johnson; b. McKinney, Tex., June 26, 1881; d. Austin, Tex., Sept. 12, 1958

BROTHER: Sam Houston (1914–   )

SISTERS: Rebekah Luruth (1910–   ); Josefa Hermine (1912–1961); Lucia Huffman (1916–   )

WIFE: Claudia Alta Taylor; b. Karnack, Tex., Dec. 22, 1912

MARRIAGE: San Antonio, Tex., Nov. 17, 1934

CHILDREN: Lynda Bird (1944–   ); Luci Baines (1947–   )

EDUCATION: Johnson City High School; Southwest Texas State Teachers College (B.S., 1930); attended Georgetown University Law School

RELIGIOUS AFFILIATION: Disciples of Christ

OCCUPATIONS BEFORE PRESIDENCY: Rancher; politician

PRE-PRESIDENTIAL OFFICES: National Youth Administration Director in Texas; Member U.S. House of Representatives; Member U.S. Senate; Vice President

MILITARY SERVICE: Lt. commander, commander, U.S. Naval Reserve (active duty 1941–1942)

AGE AT INAUGURATION: 55

FIRST ADMINISTRATION

INAUGURATION: November 22, 1963; aboard *Air Force One*, Dallas, Tex.

SECRETARY OF STATE: Dean Rusk

SECRETARY OF THE TREASURY: C. Douglas Dillon

SECRETARY OF DEFENSE: Robert S. McNamara

ATTORNEY GENERAL: Robert F. Kennedy

POSTMASTER GENERAL: John A. Gronouski

SECRETARY OF THE INTERIOR: Stewart L. Udall

SECRETARY OF AGRICULTURE: Orville L. Freeman

SECRETARY OF COMMERCE: Luther H. Hodges

SECRETARY OF LABOR: W. Willard Wirtz

SECRETARY OF HEALTH, EDUCATION, AND WELFARE: Anthony J. Celebrezze

AMBASSADOR TO THE UNITED NATIONS: Adlai E. Stevenson

88th CONGRESS (January 3, 1963–January 3, 1965):
Senate: 67 Democrats; 33 Republicans
House: 258 Democrats; 177 Republicans

ELECTION OF 1964

CANDIDATES	ELECTORAL VOTE	POPULAR VOTE
Lyndon B. Johnson Democratic	486	43,129,484
Barry M. Goldwater Republican	52	27,178,188

SECOND ADMINISTRATION

INAUGURATION: January 20, 1965; Washington, D.C.

VICE PRESIDENT: Hubert H. Humphrey

SECRETARY OF STATE: Dean Rusk

SECRETARY OF THE TREASURY: C. Douglas Dillon; Henry H. Fowler (from April 1, 1965)

SECRETARY OF DEFENSE: Robert S. McNamara; Clark M. Clifford (from March 1, 1968)

ATTORNEY GENERAL: Nicholas Katzenbach; W. Ramsey Clark (from March 10, 1967)

POSTMASTER GENERAL: John A. Gronouski; Lawrence O'Brien (from Nov. 3, 1965); W. Marvin Watson

SECRETARY OF THE INTERIOR: Stewart L. Udall

SECRETARY OF AGRICULTURE: Orville L. Freeman

SECRETARY OF COMMERCE: John T. Connor; Alexander B. Trowbridge; C. R. Smith (from May 10, 1968)

SECRETARY OF LABOR: W. Willard Wirtz

SECRETARY OF HEALTH, EDUCATION, AND WELFARE: Anthony J. Celebrezze; John W. Gardner; Wilbur J. Cohen (from March 1, 1968)

SECRETARY OF HOUSING AND URBAN DEVELOPMENT (Department created Sept. 9, 1965): Robert C. Weaver

SECRETARY OF TRANSPORTATION (Department created Oct. 15, 1966): Alan S. Boyd

AMBASSADOR TO THE UNITED NATIONS: Adlai E. Stevenson; Arthur J. Goldberg (from July 26, 1965); George Ball (from June 24, 1968)

SUPREME COURT APPOINTMENTS: Abe Fortas (1965); Thurgood Marshall (1967)

89th CONGRESS (January 3, 1965–January 3, 1967):
Senate: 68 Democrats; 32 Republicans
House: 295 Democrats; 140 Republicans

90th CONGRESS (January 3, 1967–January 3, 1969):
Senate: 64 Democrats; 36 Republicans
House: 248 Democrats; 187 Republicans

INDEX

Roman numerals refer to the volume in which the
entry appears. Arabic numbers designate the page.

190, 213–17 *passim*, 231, 232–33, 239, 251, 252, 259, 263; IV, 292, 294, 303, 314, 340, 345

California, III, 237; IV, 293, 307, 312, 313, 314, 333, 334, 348; V, 393; VI, 525

Camden, Battle of, I, 18, 38

Cameron, Simon, V, 411, 413; VI, 487

Canada, I, 32, 48; II, 137, 139, 140, 149, 152, 153; III, 255, 261; IV, 293; V, 370, 375; VIII, 705, 712

Canadian Reciprocity Treaty, V, 370, 375

Cannon, Joseph G., VIII, 704

Capitol, U.S.
building of, I, 86, 87
burning of, II, 150

Cardozo, Benjamin N., X, 878, 879

Carnegie, Andrew, VII, 598

Caroline, III, 255, 261

Carroll, Charles, III, 216

Cass, Lewis, III, 256; IV, 332, 333, 334, 338; V, 366, 379, 383

Castro, Fidel, XI, 958; XII, 1003, 1004, 1020, 1038

Cather, Willa, IX, 782

Cedar Run, Battle of, V, 433

Cermak, Anton, X, 846, 847

Chamberlain, Neville, X, 857

Champlain, Lake, I, 17; II, 153

Chancellorsville, Battle of, V, 416; VI, 500, 502, 503

Channing, William Ellery, III, 265; VII, 577

Charleston, S.C., I, 18, 39; IV, 355; V, 389, 390, 399, 419, 442

Charleston Harbor, III, 209; V, 429

Chase, Salmon P., V, 411, 413; VI, 462, 473

Château-Thierry, Battle of, IX, 739

Chattanooga, Battle of, V, 418, 432; VI, 484, 502

Cherokee Indians, III, 220, 235; V, 373

Chesapeake, II, 106, 122, 123, 139

Chesapeake and Ohio Canal, III, 192

Chiang Kai-shek, X, 890; XI, 912, 917, 937, 939

Chiari, Roberto, XII, 1038

Chicago Pullman strike, VII, 592, 606, 607; IX, 731

Chickamauga, Battle of, V, 432; VII, 546, 547

China, VIII, 642; X, 888, 890; XI, 912, 916, 917, 935, 937, 940, 941; XII, 999, 1040, 1042, 1060
Quemoy and Matsu, XI, 960, 983
See also Manchuria

Church, Frank, XII, 1042

Churchill, Winston S., X, 858–62 *passim*, 887, 890, 893; XI, 908, 909, 918, 924

Civil liberties, II, 100, 107; III, 203; X, 878, 879

Civil rights, II, 165; XI, 910, 914, 986; XII, 1005, 1021, 1034, 1037, 1040, 1042, 1047, 1058

Civil Rights Act of 1866, VI, 460, 461

Civil Rights Act of 1964, XI, 918; XII, 1037

Civil Rights Commission, XI, 957

Civil service, VI, 520, 523, 524, 526, 536; VII, 550, 554, 564, 565, 566, 569, 570, 587, 588, 600, 615, 617, 626; VIII, 704

Civil Service Commission, VI, 504; VII, 570; VIII, 679

Civil War, III, 256, 265; V, 414–19 *passim*, 430–42 *passim*; VI, 461, 484–85, 497, 500
casualties in, VI, 496
end of, V, 419
start of, V, 414, 429
See also Ulysses S. Grant, Abraham Lincoln, and individual battles and generals

Civil War pensions, VII, 588
See also Dependent Pension Act

Civil Works Administration, X, 851

Civilian Conservation Corps, X, 848, 874

Clark, George Rogers, I, 39; II, 121

Clark, James Beauchamp, VIII, 712; IX, 729, 730

Clark, William, I, 39; II, 121
See also Lewis and Clark expedition

Clay, Henry, II, 137, 164, 174, 175; III, 189, 190, 196–97, 198, 199, 208, 216, 217, 228, 237, 238, 239, 241, 263; IV, 278, 290, 291, 292, 297, 300, 309–10, 311, 316, 317; V, 424; XI, 932
and Compromise of 1850, II, 175; III, 188; IV, 333–34, 340–45
and Missouri Compromise, II, 165, 175
See also John Quincy Adams

Clay, Lucretia, II, 175

Clayton Antitrust Act, IX, 748

Clayton-Bulwer Treaty, IV, 334; V, 370, 388

Clemenceau, Georges, IX, 740, 741, 759, 760, 761

Clemens, Samuel L., VI, 487, 492; VII, 556, 578

Cleveland, Frances Folsom, VII, 588, 596–97

Cleveland, Grover, VII, 583–609 *passim*, VIII, 715
appraisal of, VII, 588, 592, 607
birth and early life, VII, 583, 584
and cancer operation, VII, 590
and civil service reform, VII, 587, 600
death of, VII, 592
and 1884 election, VII, 578, 583, 586, 587, 589, 594, 595
and 1888 election, VII, 587, 588, 600, 615, 620
and 1892 election, VII, 589, 590, 618
and 1896 election, VII, 592
Facts in Summary, VII, 608–9
and gold standard, VII, 588, 590, 591, 592, 607
and Hawaii annexation dispute,

VII, 591, 592, 607, 618
and Interstate Commerce Act, VII, 587, 600
and labor disputes, VII, 592, 606, 607
marriage of, VII, 588, 596, 597
and "Mugwumps" in 1884 election, VII, 586, 587
nonconsecutive terms of, VII, 583
and party control, VII, 587–88
and patronage, VII, 587–88, 590, 600
pre-presidential politics and offices, VII, 578, 584–86, 595
as President
first term, VII, 587–88, 596–600
second term, VII, 589–92 *passim*, 606–7
and repeal of Sherman Silver-Purchase Act, VII, 590–91, 606
and repeal of Tenure of Office Act, VII, 600
and "silver letter" of 1891, VII, 589
and Tammany Hall, VII, 585–88 *passim*, 595, 611
and tariff reduction, VII, 588, 592, 600, 615
and Treasury surplus, VII, 602–3
and Venezuelan-British border dispute, VII, 591, 592, 607
and veto, VII, 587, 600

Clinton, DeWitt, II, 138, 147; III, 250, 258

Clinton, George, II, 106, 138, 146

Clinton, Sir Henry, I, 18

Coal industry, IX, 773; XI, 911–12
See also Labor and labor unions

Cohn, Roy M., XI, 956, 973

Cold war, X, 860; XI, 908, 909, 913, 928, 929, 953–60 *passim*, 977; XII, 1017

Colfax, Schuyler, VI, 486, 490, 508

Colombia, VIII, 668, 691

Commerce, I, 24, 25, 46; II, 105, 118; III, 187, 238, 241, 260; IV, 349; VI, 487; X, 851

Commission on Efficiency and Economy, VIII, 704

Commission for Relief in Belgium, X, 816–17

Communications Act, X, 851

Communism, X, 820; XI, 915, 916, 969, 983; XII, 1038–42 *passim*

Compromise of 1850, II, 175; III, 265; IV, 322, 329, 333, 334, 341, 345–46, 348, 355; V, 365, 373, 388
See also Fugitive Slave Law

Conant, James B., XI, 927

Concord, Mass., I, 75

Confederate States of America, V, 390, 411, 413, 429, 432, 437; V, 459, 485
See also Civil War

Confederation, Articles of. *See* Articles of Confederation

CIO Political Action Committee, X, 873

Conkling, Roscoe, VI, 487, 523–24, 526, 536, 537; VII, 549, 550,

Dependent Pension Act, VII, 616, 622

Depressions, II, 138, 165; III, 218, 241, 253, 254, 255; IV, 347
  1930's Depression, IX, 782; X, 815, 818–22 *passim*, 826, 827, 844, 845–51 *passim*, 870, 883, 894
  See also individual Panics, Herbert Hoover, Franklin Delano Roosevelt

Derna, Tripoli, II, 105, 122

Desegregation, XI, 957, 980, 985; XII, 1005, 1040, 1041, 1054, 1058

Deseret, IV, 333; V, 388

Detroit, I, 39; II, 139; III, 250; XII, 1042

Dewey, George, VIII, 641, 649, 651, 653

Dewey, John, IX, 750

Dewey, Thomas E., X, 861, 862; XI, 914, 929, 931

Díaz, Porfirio, VI, 525

Dickinson, Charles, III, 211

Diem, Ngo Dinh, XII, 1005, 1039, 1041

Dingley Tariff, VIII, 639, 640, 644

Dinwiddie, Robert, I, 12, 13, 14, 28

District of Columbia, II, 125; III, 254; IV, 333; V, 406, 407, 415; IX, 746
  See also Washington, D.C.

Dix, Dorothea, VII, 577

Dodge, Joseph M., XI, 972

Doheny, Edward L., IX, 773

Dole, Sanford B., VII, 618

"Dollar Diplomacy," VIII, 704–5; X, 841

Dominican Republic, VI, 488, 489, 504, 509; VIII, 669; XII, 1040–41, 1056, 1057

Donelson, Emily, III, 218

Dorchester Heights, Mass., I, 16, 32, 49

Dorr's Rebellion, IV, 296

Dorsey, Stephen, VII, 567, 569

Douglas, Stephen A., IV, 349; V, 366, 373, 379, 384–89 *passim*, 398, 399, 408–11 *passim*, 424, 426; VI, 457
  and Compromise of 1850, IV, 333, 334; V, 424
  and Kansas-Nebraska Act, V, 368, 378, 408, 409, 424

Douglas, William O., XI, 908, 915

Douglass, Frederick, V, 396

Downie, George, II, 153

Draft, the, IX, 756; X, 857; XI, 932

Dred Scott decision, V, 385, 396, 408, 409, 424

Dreiser, Theodore, IX, 783

Duane, William J., III, 218

Dulles, John Foster, XI, 955, 956, 959, 972, 977, 982, 985

Dumbarton Oaks Conference, X, 861

Dunmore, 4th Earl of, II, 97, 98, 112

Dupuy de Lôme, Stanislas, VIII, 640

Durkin, Martin P., XI, 972, 973

E

Early, Jubal A., V, 433

Eastern Europe, X, 860; XI, 912, 959

Eaton, John Henry, III, 213, 215, 230–31, 252

Eaton, Margaret O'Neale, III, 215, 218, 230–31, 252

Eaton, William, II, 105, 122

Eaton affair, III, 252
  See also Andrew Jackson, Martin Van Buren

Economic Development Administration, XII, 1054

Economy Act of 1933, X, 848

Eden, Anthony, X, 890; XI, 976

Edison, Thomas, VI, 526; VII, 605; IX, 778

Education, III, 191, 220, 264; IX, 750
  federal aid to, III, 191, 192, 251; XI, 910, 957, 971, 980; XII, 1040, 1051, 1054

Egypt, XI, 960; XII, 1042

Einstein, Albert, XI, 926

Eisenhower, Arthur, XI, 950

Eisenhower, David Jacob, XI, 950, 951, 952

Eisenhower, Dwight David, X, 822, 886, 890; XI, 914, 918, 949–89 *passim*; XII, 999, 1019, 1034, 1035, 1037, 1039
  appraisal of, XI, 952, 953, 954, 960, 964, 986
  birth and early life, XI, 949–50, 962, 963
  and Cabinet, XI, 972, 973
  and Chinese Communists, XI, 960, 969, 983
  and Congress, XI, 986
  criticism of, XI, 954, 959, 960, 972, 973, 975, 980, 986
  and desegregation, XI, 957, 980
  domestic policies, XI, 973, 980, 986
  Facts in Summary, XI, 988–89
  Farewell Address, XI, 960, 986
  and foreign affairs, XI, 956, 957–58, 959, 960, 977–78, 983, 985
  and Hungarian Revolt, XI, 959, 978
  illnesses, XI, 951–52, 957, 958, 959, 983
  and Korean War, XI, 953–54, 955–56, 969, 972
  and McCarthyism, XI, 939, 954, 956–57, 969
  marriage of, XI, 952, 963
  and 1948 election, XI, 953, 967
  and 1952 election, XI, 935, 953, 954, 967, 968, 969, 971; XII, 1003
  and 1956 election, XI, 956, 958
  and NATO, XI, 953, 967, 983
  as President, XI, 954–60 *passim*, 973, 976–86 *passim*
  as president of Columbia, XI, 953, 966, 967
  pre-World War II military career, XI, 949–51*passim*, 962
  and space program, XI, 959, 980

and universal disarmament, XI, 957, 958
  and World War II, XI, 935, 949–53 *passim*, 963, 964, 966

Eisenhower, Earl, XI, 950

Eisenhower, Edgar, XI, 950, 952

Eisenhower, Ida Elizabeth Stover, XI, 950, 951, 952, 963

Eisenhower, John, XI, 952, 982

Eisenhower, Mamie Geneva Doud, XI, 952, 955, 963

Eisenhower, Milton, XI, 950, 963

Eisenhower, Roy, XI, 950

Eisenhower Doctrine, XI, 960

Elections and election campaigns. *See* Facts in Summary for each President and individual candidates

Electoral Commission, VI, 522

Eliot, Charles W., VII, 586, 624

Elk Hills oil leases, IX, 767, 768

Elkins Act, VIII, 667

Emancipation Proclamation, V, 416, 438–39
  Preliminary Emancipation Proclamation, V, 416, 439

Embargoes, II, 120, 123, 136
  Embargo Act, II, 106–7, 122; III, 187

Emergency Farm Mortgage Act, X, 849

Emerson, Ralph Waldo, V, 376, 377, 387

Erie, Lake, I, 28; II, 139, 153

Evarts, William M., VI, 523, 526, 532, 534

Everett, Edward, V, 416–17

Ewell, Richard S., VI, 500

Ewing, Thomas, IV, 285

Executive Mansion, I, 22, 23
  See also White House

Expansion, II, 137, 148, 160, 164, 171; III, 189, 191; IV, 276–77, 281, 307, 316, 332; V, 374–75, 388; VI, 487; VII, 618; VIII, 650, 655
  See also American imperialism

Expedition Act, VIII, 667

F

Fair Deal, X, 872; XI, 913

Fair Labor Standards Act, X, 856

Fair Oaks, Battle of, V, 434

Fairbanks, Charles W., VIII, 673

Fairfax, George, I, 11

Fairfax, Lord Thomas, I, 11

Fairfax, Sally, I, 11, 14, 15

Fairfax Resolutions, II, 112

Fall, Albert B., IX, 767, 768, 772, 773, 774

Farley, James A., X, 844, 845, 846, 852, 868, 882

Farm Credit Administration, X, 850–51

Farmers, VII, 585, 611, 616, 618; IX, 773, 795; X, 818, 825, 826, 848–49, 856; XI, 930

Farmers' Alliances, VII, 617

Farragut, David, V, 416, 433

Faubus, Orval, XI, 957, 980

Faulkner, William, XI, 974

H

773, 774, 784, 785
death of, IX, 768, 774, 784, 785, 792
as editor of Marion *Star*, IX, 769–70
Facts in Summary, IX, 786–87
marriage of, IX, 770
and Nan Britton, IX, 771, 772, 774
and naval disarmament conference, IX, 774, 780
and 1920 election, IX, 742, 771, 772, 773, 775, 776; X, 817
and "normalcy," IX, 771–72, 773, 774, 778, 792
pre-presidential politics and offices, IX, 770–72
as President, IX, 767–68, 773–74, 778–81, 784–85
Harlan, John Marshall, VIII, 714, 715
Harmon, Judson, IX, 729, 730
Harpers Ferry, Va., V, 376, 387, 394, 416
Harriman, W. Averell, X, 890; XI, 906, 909; XII, 1014
Harrison, Anna Symmes, IV, 276, 277, 285
Harrison, Benjamin (1726–1791), IV, 275; VII, 612
Harrison, Benjamin, IV, 277; VII, 611–29 *passim*; VIII, 674, 679
appraisal of, VII, 612
birth and early life, VII, 612
Cabinet of, VII, 617
and Chilean dispute, VII, 618
and civil service reform, VII, 615, 617, 626
in Civil War, VII, 613, 614
death of, VII, 618
and 1888 election, VII, 588, 600, 611, 615, 620
and 1892 election, VII, 589, 618, 620, 626
Facts in Summary, VII, 628–29
and Hawaii annexation dispute, VII, 618
and Italian government, VII, 618
and McKinley Tariff, VII, 617
marriage of, VII, 612, 618
and party politics, VII, 612, 613, 614, 621, 626
pre-presidential politics and offices, VII, 612–15 *passim*
as President, VII, 611–12, 615–18 *passim*, 621–23 *passim*, 626
and social problems of industrial growth, VII, 611–12, 616–17
and U.S. Treasury, VII, 602–3
and Venezuelan-British border dispute, VII, 618
Harrison, Caroline Scott, VII, 612, 618, 620, 622
Harrison, Elizabeth Irwin, VII, 612
Harrison, John Scott, VII, 612, 613
Harrison, Russell Benjamin, VII, 620
Harrison, William Henry, IV, 275–87 *passim*; VII, 611, 612, 620; VIII, 700
birth and early life, IV, 275–76
death of, IV, 278, 284, 285, 289

and 1836 election, III, 253, 259; IV, 278, 283, 290
and 1840 election, III, 251, 256; IV, 275–85 *passim*
Facts in Summary, IV, 286–87
inauguration of, IV, 284, 285
and Indians, II, 137–38; IV, 276, 277, 281
and Northwest Territory, IV, 276, 277
pre-presidential offices, II, 137–38; IV, 276, 278, 281
as President, IV, 278, 284–85
and slavery, IV, 276, 278
and Tippecanoe, Battle of, II, 137–38; IV, 277, 278, 281
and War of 1812, II, 139; IV, 277–78, 281
Hartford Convention, II, 155
Harvard University, I, 16, 62; II, 97; III, 186, 188, 192; VII, 624; VIII, 662, 676, 694; X, 838, 839, 864, 865, 879; XI, 913, 933, 975; XII, 995–99 *passim*, 1002, 1008, 1014, 1015, 1022
Harvey, George, IX, 727, 728
Harvie, Colonel John, II, 96
Havana Harbor, VIII, 640, 649
Hawaii, IV, 349; VII, 616, 618; VIII, 641, 650; XI, 988
Hawley-Smoot Tariff, X, 820
Hawthorne, Nathaniel, I, 10; V, 366, 367, 370, 376, 377
Hay, Eliza Monroe, II, 172
Hay, John M., V, 403; VIII, 642, 653
Hay-Hernan Convention, VIII, 668
Hay-Pauncefote Treaty, VIII, 653, 705
second Hay-Pauncefote Treaty, VIII, 668
Hayes, Fanny, VI, 533
Hayes, Fanny Arabella, VI, 518
Hayes, Lucy Ware Webb, VI, 518, 519, 526, 528, 532, 533
Hayes, Rutherford, VI, 517
Hayes, Rutherford Birchard, VI, 517–39 *passim*; VII, 545, 555; VIII, 636
appraisal of, VI, 517, 526
and assertion of presidential authority, VI, 524
birth and early life, VI, 517–18
Cabinet of, VI, 523, 534
and Chinese immigration, VI, 525–26, 539
and civil service reform, VI, 520, 523, 524, 526, 536; VII, 565
death of, VI, 526
and 1876 election, VI, 519–20, 521, 522, 526, 528, 530–31
Facts in Summary, VI, 538–39
inauguration of, VI, 522
marriage of, VI, 518, 528
and N.Y. Custom House, VI, 523–24, 536–37; VII, 565
and pre-presidential politics, VI, 519, 528
as President, VI, 517, 522–26 *passim*, 532–37 *passim*
and railroad strike, VI, 524, 525
and Reconstruction, VI, 517, 523, 526

and reform in government, VI, 520, 523–24, 526, 531, 532
and sister, VI, 518
and Union, VI, 517
in Union army, VI, 519, 528; VIII, 636
and U.S. monetary problems, VI, 524
and veto, VI, 524, 525–26, 539
Hayes, Scott, VI, 533
Hayes, Sophia Birchard, VI, 517–18
Hearst, William Randolph, VIII, 646, 712; X, 845
Heaton, Leonard, XI, 957
Hemingway, Ernest, XI, 975
Henderson, John B., VI, 463, 477
Hendricks, Thomas A., VII, 589
Henry, Patrick, II, 100, 112, 113, 160
Hermitage, The, III, 220, 222, 227, 228, 244, 245
Herndon, William H., V, 403, 422
Herold, David, V, 445
Herter, Christian, XI, 982
Hessians, I, 17, 32; II, 161
Hillman, Sidney, X, 873
Hirohito, Emperor, X, 858
Hiroshima, XI, 910
Hiss, Alger, XI, 936
Hitler, Adolf, II, 177; X, 832, 852, 856–58 *passim*, 880, 886, 890; XI, 928
Hoban, James, I, 86
Hobart, Garret A., VIII, 638, 639, 645
Hobby, Oveta Culp, XI, 972
Hoffa, James, XII, 1014
Holmes, Oliver Wendell, Jr., VIII, 715; X, 878
Home Owners Loan Corporation, X, 849
Homestead Act, V, 411; VI, 456, 457, 487
Homesteaders, VII, 616
Hood, John Bell, V, 419, 432; VI, 502, 503
Hooker, Joseph, V, 416; VII, 614
Hoover, Allan Henry, X, 816
Hoover, Herbert Clark, VIII, 717; IX, 785, 794; X, 815–35 *passim*, 846, 847
appraisal of, X, 822
birth and early life, X, 816, 822–25 *passim*
and bonus marchers, X, 815–16, 828
conservatism of, X, 817–22 *passim*, 825, 826
death of, X, 822
and Depression, III, 255; X, 815, 818–22 *passim*, 826, 829
and European relief in World War I and World War II; X, 816, 817, 822, 825, 832
Facts in Summary, X, 834–35
and federal dole, X, 820–21, 825, 829
and foreign affairs, X, 820, 829
and 1928 election, X, 815, 818, 827
and 1932 election, X, 821, 822
post-presidential offices, X, 822, 832

and Supreme Court, II, 108
and University of Virginia, II, 107–8, 126, 127, 140
as Vice President, I, 67–68; II, 102
and war with Tripoli, II, 105
writings by, II, 98, 102, 107, 111, 126
See also Monticello
Jenner, William, XI, 969
Job Corps, XII, 1054
Johnson, Andrew, VI, 455–79 *passim*; VII, 564
abuse by press, VI, 460, 468, 470
accession of, VI, 458, 468
and Army Appropriations Act, VI, 461
birth and early life, VI, 456, 467
and Cabinet, VI, 459, 464, 472, 534
and Congress, VI, 455–64 *passim*, 468, 470
and the Constitution, VI, 455, 460, 463, 464
death of, VI, 464
and 1860 election, VI, 457
and 1864 election, V, 418; VI, 458, 468
and 1866 congressional elections, VI, 460–61
Facts in Summary, VI, 478–79
impeachment of, V, 397; VI, 455, 461, 462–63, 472–75 *passim*, 487, 534
and Lee's surrender, VI, 486
and Lincoln assassination plot, V, 445; VI, 468
marriage of, VI, 456, 467
and Mexico, VI, 464, 471
pre-presidential politics and offices, VI, 456–58, 464–68 *passim*, 477
as President, VI, 455, 458–64 *passim*, 468–77 *passim*
and press interviews, VI, 474–75
and purchase of Alaska, VI, 464, 470, 473
and Reconstruction, VI, 455, 458–59, 468
and secession, VI, 457–58
and slavery, VI, 457, 460
and the Union, VI, 456, 457, 458
and veto, IV, 296; VI, 456, 460, 461, 464, 470
as Vice President, VI, 458, 468
vindication of, VI, 464, 477
Johnson, Andrew (1852–1879), VI, 458
Johnson, Claudia Alta Taylor ("Lady Bird"), XII, 1030, 1034, 1044, 1045, 1046, 1048, 1056
Johnson, Eliza McCardle, VI, 456, 457, 458, 466, 467, 476, 477
Johnson, Hiram, IX, 741, 762, 794
Johnson, Luci Baines, XII, 1030, 1036
Johnson, Lynda Bird, XII, 1030, 1036
Johnson, Lyndon Baines, XI, 986, XII, 1001, 1002, 1006, 1024, 1029–63 *passim*
accession of, XII, 1034, 1048, 1049
appraisal of, XII, 1029

birth and early life, XII, 1029–30
and civil rights, XII, 1032, 1034, 1035, 1038, 1040
domestic policies, XII, 1035–36, 1038–39, 1041, 1042, 1049, 1051, 1054–56 *passim*, 1060
and Dominican Republic, XII, 1038–39, 1056
Facts in Summary, XII, 1062–63
foreign policy, XII, 1036–42 *passim*, 1051, 1060–61
and Glassboro talks, XII, 1040
and Great Society, XII, 1029, 1052, 1054
illnesses, XII, 1033
as Majority Leader, XII, 1032–33, 1047
marriage of, XII, 1030, 1044
and Mideast Crisis, XII, 1040
and military preparedness, XII, 1031, 1032, 1033
and 1960 election, XII, 1001, 1002, 1034, 1046
and 1964 election, XII, 1038, 1041, 1052, 1053
and Panama, XII, 1036, 1051
pre-presidential politics and offices, XII, 1030–34 *passim*, 1044, 1047
as President, XII, 1034–42 *passim*, 1047–61 *passim*
and railroad dispute, XII, 1035
as Vice President, XII, 1002, 1006, 1034, 1047
and Vietnam, XII, 1032, 1036–42 *passim*, 1060–61
in World War II, XII, 1031
Johnson, Rebekah Baines, XII, 1029, 1030, 1045
Johnson, Richard M., III, 251; IV, 278
Johnson, Samuel Ealy, XII, 1029–30
Johnson, Samuel Ealy, Jr., XII, 1029, 1030
Johnson, William, VI, 467
Johnston, Alvanley, XI, 911
Johnston, Harriet L., V, 401
Johnston, Joseph, VI, 497, 498, 499, 502
Jones, John Paul, I, 38
Jones, Joseph, II, 160, 161
Juárez, Benito, VI, 471
Judicial review, doctrine of, II, 113
Judiciary Act, II, 105, 125

K

Kane, Thomas L., V, 388
Kansas, V, 368, 370, 378–79, 384, 385–86, 387, 412, 424.
Kansas-Nebraska Act, V, 368, 378, 397, 408, 424
Kearney, Denis, VI, 539
Kefauver, Estes, XII, 1000, 1011
Keller, Helen, XII, 1022
Kellogg, Frank B., IX, 795, 796
Kellogg-Briand Pact, IX, 796, 802; X, 830
Kelly, John, VII, 586, 595

Kendall, Amos, III, 216, 218, 240
Kennedy, Caroline, XII, 1001, 1019
Kennedy, Edward M., XII, 997
Kennedy, Eunice, XII, 997, 1008
Kennedy, Jacqueline, XII, 998, 999, 1003–4, 1005, 1006, 1010, 1018, 1019, 1024, 1026, 1048
Kennedy, Jean, XII, 997
Kennedy, John F., II, 126; VIII, 665; X, 835; XI, 932, 944, 971, 986; XII, 995–1029 *passim*, 1036–40 *passim*, 1058
and Alliance for Progress, XII, 1003, 1017
assassination of, XII, 1006, 1024, 1025, 1026, 1048, 1049
and Bay of Pigs, XII, 1003, 1017
birth and early life, XII, 995–98 *passim*, 1008, 1009, 1010–11
and civil rights, XII, 1005, 1021
in Congress, XII, 999–1000
and Cuban Missile Crisis, II, 177; XII, 1004, 1020, 1021
domestic programs, 1004, 1005, 1021
Facts in Summary, XII, 1026–27
and family, XII, 996, 1008
foreign affairs, XII, 1002–6 *passim*, 1016, 1017, 1021
illnesses, XII, 998–99, 1000, 1001
inauguration of, XII, 996, 1002, 1019
marriage of, XII, 999, 1010, 1026
and 1956 election, XII, 1000, 1011
and 1960 election, XII, 1000–1002, 1003, 1007, 1012
and 1962 congressional elections, XII, 1004
and nuclear test ban treaty, XII, 1004, 1021
and Peace Corps, XII, 1002–3, 1017
as President, XII, 1002–6 *passim*, 1017–26 *passim*
and religion, XII, 1001, 1002, 1012
in U.S. Navy, XII, 995–96, 997, 1009, 1011
and Vietnam, XII, 1005–6, 1039
Kennedy, John F., Jr., XII, 1002, 1019
Kennedy, Joseph P., XII, 996–99 *passim*, 1008, 1009
Kennedy, Joseph P., Jr., XII, 996–97, 998, 999, 1008
Kennedy, Kathleen, XII, 997, 1008
Kennedy, Patricia, XII, 997
Kennedy, Patrick J., XII, 996, 1008
Kennedy, Robert F., XII, 997, 999, 1000, 1001, 1005, 1014, 1042
Kennedy, Rose Fitzgerald, XII, 996, 1008
Kentucky, I, 39, 82; II, 103; III, 216; V, 385
Kentucky Resolutions, II, 104
Key, Francis Scott, II, 140
Khrushchev, Nikita S., X, 894–95; XI, 958, 959, 960, 983; XII, 1003, 1004, 1016, 1017, 1020
King, Ernest J., X, 860, 888, 890

King, Martin Luther, Jr., XII, 1058
King, Rufus, II, 106, 142, 164, 171
King, William R., V, 369, 371
Kleberg, Richard M., XII, 1032
Know-Nothing party, IV, 331, 332, 350, 356; V, 369
Knox, Frank, X, 889
Knox, Henry, I, 44, 49
Knox, Philander C., VIII, 704
Knudsen, William S., X, 860
Korea, XI, 905, 906, 917, 918, 940
Korean War, XI, 917-18, 939, 940, 941, 943, 953-54, 955-56, 969, 972, 977; XII, 1034
Kosygin, Aleksei, XII, 1042
Krug, Julius A., XI, 911, 912
Ku-Klux Klan, VI, 464, 489, 507
Ku Klux Klan, IX, 751, 774, 793, 803
Ky, Nguyen Cao, XII, 1041

L

Labor and labor unions, VI, 524, 525; VII, 585, 592, 616, 617; VIII, 667, 685; IX, 731, 773; X, 851, 856; XI, 908, 911; XII, 1037-38
See also individual labor leaders and unions
Lafayette, Marquis de, II, 101, 116, 161, 166, 173
La Follette, Robert M., VIII, 665; IX, 737-38, 741, 794, 795
La Guardia, Fiorello, IX, 757; X, 831
Landon, Alfred M., X, 854, 855
Lansing, Robert, IX, 737, 739, 742
Laos, XII, 1003, 1016, 1017
Latin America, II, 166, 176; XII, 1003, 1017, 1060
See also individual countries
Lattimore, Owen, XI, 916
Law, George, IV, 355
Lawrence, Ernest Orlando, XI, 927
Lawrence, James, II, 139
League of Nations, VIII, 674; IX, 739-42 passim, 762, 771, 773; X, 820, 845
See also Woodrow Wilson
Leahy, William D., X, 860, 888
Lebanon, XI, 960
Lecompton, Kan., V, 368, 386
Lecompton constitution, V, 386, 387, 389, 424
Lee, Charles, I, 18, 35, 37
Lee, Richard Henry, II, 98, 113
Lee, Robert E., V, 414-18 passim, 432, 449; VI, 485, 486, 497-503 passim; VIII, 554
Lehman, Herbert H., X, 845
Leigh, Benjamin, IV, 290
Lemmon slave case, VI, 534
Lenroot, Irvine H., IX, 798
Leopard, H.M.S., II, 123
Lesseps, Ferdinand Marie de, VI, 525
Lewis, John L., XI, 911-12, 942
Lewis, Meriwether, II, 106, 121
Lewis and Clark expedition, I, 39; II, 106, 121

Lexington, Mass., I, 75; II, 98
Liberal Republican party, VI, 489, 490, 534; VII, 566; VIII, 647
Liliuokalani, Queen, VII, 616, 618
Lincoln, Abraham, III, 256; IV, 276, 332, 350; V, 396, 403-49 passim; VI, 458
abuse by press, V, 415, 439
and Ann Rutledge, V, 405-6
appraisal of, V, 403, 420
assassination of, V, 403, 420, 445, 447; VI, 468, 485
birth and early life, V, 404-5, 438, 440
Cabinet of, V, 412-15 passim, 420, 429; VI, 472
and Civil War, V, 414, 415, 416, 429-42 passim; VI, 458, 481, 484, 485
and 1860 election, V, 370, 389, 399, 409, 411, 423, 426, 427
and 1864 election, V, 417-21 passim, 433, 440; VI, 468
and Emancipation Proclamation, V, 415, 416, 438, 439, 442
Facts in Summary, V, 448-49
funeral of, IV, 350; V, 420, 447
Gettysburg Address, V, 416-17
inaugurations, V, 412-13, 427; VI, 458, 465
marriage of, V, 406
and Mexican War, V, 407
pre-presidential politics and offices, IV, 332; V, 405-11 passim, 423
as President, V, 413-20 passim, 427-47 passim
and Reconstruction, V, 419-20
and slavery, IV, 346; V, 405-18 passim, 424, 427, 438, 439
speeches by, V, 408-9, 410, 412-13, 419, 442
and the Union, V, 408, 413-18 passim, 437, 442; VI, 468
Lincoln, Edward Baker, V, 407, 423
Lincoln, Mary Todd, V, 406, 411, 414-15, 420, 422, 423, 441
Lincoln, Nancy Hanks, V, 404
Lincoln, Robert Todd, V, 406-7, 420, 423, 441; VII, 575
Lincoln, Sarah Bush Johnston, V, 404
Lincoln, Thomas, V, 404, 405
Lincoln, Thomas ("Tad"), V, 407, 413, 423, 441
Lincoln, William Wallace, V, 407, 414, 423
Lincoln-Douglas debates, V, 409, 424
Lindbergh, Charles A., VIII, 674; IX, 805
Livingston, Edward, III, 213, 240
Livingston, Robert R., I, 21; II, 98, 105, 115, 120, 163, 168
Lloyd George, David, IX, 740, 741, 760, 761
Locke, John, II, 102, 134
Lockwood, Belva Ann, VII, 594
Lodge, Henry Cabot, VII, 586; VIII, 679, 681, 706; IX, 742, 785, 789; X, 817; XII, 999
and League of Nations, VIII, 674; IX, 740, 741, 742

Lodge, Henry Cabot II, XI, 954, 972; XII. 999, 1011
Log cabin campaign, III, 256; IV, 275, 276, 283
London International Monetary and Economic Conference, X, 851-52
Long, Huey, X, 831
Long, John, VIII, 663, 664, 681
Long Island, Battle of, I, 16
Longfellow, Henry Wadsworth, VII, 556
Longstreet, James, VI, 500
Louis Napoleon, IV, 349; VI, 464, 471
Louis XVI, II, 116, 117, 162
Louis Philippe, III, 216
Louisiana, I, 39; II, 105, 168; V, 389, 390, 419-20, 439; VI, 520-21, 522, 523, 531
Louisiana Purchase, II, 105-6, 118, 119, 137, 165; III, 187
Lusitania, VIII, 694; IX, 736, 737, 752
Lyon, Mary, III, 264
Lyon, Matthew, I, 82, 83

M

McAdoo, William G., IX, 734, 747, 748, 793; X, 868
MacArthur, Douglas, IX, 757; X, 816, 828, 886, 890; XI, 905, 917-18, 940, 941, 943, 953, 962, 963
McCarran Internal Security Act, XI, 916-17
McCarthy, Joseph, XI, 915-16, 917, 918, 937, 939, 954, 956-57, 969, 973; XII, 1000
McClellan, George B., IV, 350; V, 414, 416, 417, 418, 440; VI, 484, 500, 502, 503
McDonald, John, VI, 491
Macdonough, Thomas, II, 153
McGovern, George, XII, 1041-42
McHenry, James, I, 26
McKay, Douglas, XI, 972
McKinley, Ida Saxton, VIII, 636, 637, 642
McKinley, William, VIII, 635-59 passim, 661, 663
assassination of, VIII, 642, 656-57, 683
birth and early life, VIII, 635-36
and Boxer Rebellion, VIII, 642, 650
in Civil War, VIII, 636
and 1896 election, VIII, 637, 638, 644, 645
and expansion, VIII, 641, 650
Facts in Summary, VIII, 658-59
and gold standard, VIII, 638, 642, 644
and labor disputes, VIII, 636-37
marriage of, VIII, 636
and 1900 election, VIII, 642, 650, 656, 665, 682
and Philippine annexation, VIII, 641-42, 651
pre-presidential politics and offices, VIII, 636, 637-38

N

S

T

Venezuela, VII, 591; VIII, 669
Veterans
  Civil War, VII, 615, 616
  World War I, X, 815–16
Veterans Bureau Frauds, IX, 767, 773, 774
Vice Presidency, I, 66, 67
  See also Facts in Summary for each President and individual Vice Presidents
Vicksburg, siege of, V, 416; VI, 484, 497, 498–99, 502
Vietnam, XI, 956, 976, 977; XII, 1005–6, 1015, 1034, 1038–42 *passim*, 1060, 1061
Villa, Francisco ("Pancho"), IX, 752, 753
Vinson, Fred, XI, 985
Virgin Islands. *See* Danish West Indies
Virginia, I, 39, 41, 49; II, 97–98, 112; V, 414, 429
Virginia Committee of Correspondence, I, 75; II, 97
Virginia Constitutional Convention, II, 166
Virginia Convention of 1776, II, 135
Virginia Declaration of Rights, II, 112, 135
Virginia House of Burgesses, I, 15, 31; II, 97, 112, 113
Virginia House of Delegates, II, 99, 100, 112; IV, 290
Virginia Ratification Convention, I, 49; II, 136
Virginia Resolutions, II, 136, 140
Voorhees, Daniel W., VII, 590
Voting Rights Act of 1965, XII, 1040, 1054

W

Wade-Davis bill, V, 419
Wagner-Connery National Labor Relations Act, X, 851, 856
Waite, Morrison R., VI, 509
Wake Island, VIII, 641, 651
Walker, James, X, 845
Walker, Robert, VIII, 638
Walker, Robert J., V, 385, 386
Walker, William, V, 370, 375
Walker Tariff of 1846, IV, 314
Wallace, Henry, X, 853, 882, 883; XI, 908, 912, 914, 923, 942
Wallace, William, VII, 613
Wanamaker, John, VII, 615; VIII, 679
War Industries Board, IX, 756
War of 1812, II, 120, 138, 139–40, 150, 152, 153, 155, 160, 163, 171; III, 188, 195, 196, 211, 250; IV, 277–78
Ward, Ferdinand, VI, 492, 512
Warren, Earl, XI, 985; XII, 1049
Warren Commission, XI, 985; XII, 1049
Washburne, Elihu B., VI, 487
Washington, Augustine, I, 10, 11, 28
Washington, Augustine, Jr., I, 10
Washington, Booker T., VII, 625;

VIII, 670, 671
Washington, Charles, I, 10
Washington, D.C., I, 24, 52, 53, 56, 86; II, 102, 104, 139–40, 164, 172, 173; IV, 329; V, 414; VI, 517; VIII, 710
  burning of, II, 150
Washington, George, I, 9–59 *passim*, 65, 68, 70; II, 102, 106, 112, 116, 120, 133, 142, 160, 162, 165, 171; III, 186, 187, 207, 210, 220, 249; IV, 332; V, 390, 410; IX, 759
  appraisal of, I, 9, 10, 18, 26
  birth and early life, I, 10, 11–12, 28
  Cabinet appointments, I, 22, 26; II, 102
  and Conway Cabal, I, 19
  criticism of, I, 9, 18, 21, 24, 25, 26
  death of, I, 43, 52, 53; II, 162–63
  as delegate to Continental Congress, I, 15
  and Edmond Genêt, I, 24–25
  Facts in Summary, I, 58–59
  Farewell Address, I, 26
  first inauguration, I, 21, 44, 45
  and Jay's Treaty, I, 23, 24, 25
  legends about, I, 10
  life at Mount Vernon, I, 14–15, 42
  marriage of, I, 14
  personality and character of, I, 12, 18, 19
  physical attributes of, I, 11–12, 55
  political philosophy of, I, 19, 22, 23
  pre-Revolutionary military career, I, 12, 13, 14, 15, 28
  as President, I, 21–26 *passim*, 44–53 *passim*
  as president of Constitutional Convention, I, 20
  in Revolutionary War, I, 15–19, 31–41 *passim*; II, 139, 161, 168
  and Sally Fairfax, I, 14
  and 1789 election, I, 20
  and 1792 election, I, 24
  and slavery, I, 15
  and U.S. financial system, I, 24, 46
  and Whisky Rebellion, I, 24, 50
Washington, John Augustine, I, 10
Washington, Lawrence, I, 10, 11, 12, 28, 42
Washington, Martha Dandridge Custis, I, 14, 21, 23, 31, 42, 43, 52, 53
Washington, Mary Ball, I, 10, 11, 28
Washington, Samuel, I, 10
Washington Armament Conference, IX, 774, 780, 781; X, 830
Washington Monument, I, 56; IV, 334
Watts race riot, XII, 1057
Wealth Tax Act, X, 851
Weaver, James B., VII, 554, 589, 618
Weaver, Robert C., XII, 1005

Webster, Daniel, III, 189, 207, 215, 216, 217, 218, 239, 259; IV, 278, 285, 290–94 *passim*, 300, 333, 338, 340, 345, 348, 349; VI, 517; VII, 545
Webster, Fletcher, IV, 289, 291
Webster-Ashburton Treaty, III, 255; IV, 293, 300
Weed, Thurlow, IV, 330, 346, 347, 348, 350; VII, 564
Weeks, Sinclair, XI, 972
Weems, Mason L., I, 10; V, 405
Welles, Gideon, V, 413; VI, 455, 462, 464
West, the, I, 25; II, 106, 121, 122; III, 237, 238, 254; IV, 307, 322, 349; VI, 487; VII, 626
West Point, I, 49; VI, 495; XI, 949, 963, 984
Westmoreland, William C., XII, 1041
Wheeler, William A., VI, 521, 530, 533
Wheeler-Rayburn Act, X, 851
Whig party, II, 175; III, 219, 251–59 *passim*; IV, 275, 276, 278, 283, 289–96 *passim*, 308, 309, 314, 316, 317, 330, 332, 339, 341, 346–50 *passim*, 356; V, 367; VI, 457
Whisky Rebellion, I, 24, 38, 50, 51
White, Edward D., VIII, 715
White, Edward H., XII, 1056, 1057
White, Henry, IX, 739
White, Hugh L., III, 259; IV, 290
White House, the, I, 22, 70, 78, 86, 87; II, 106, 136, 145, 164, 170, 172, 173; III, 190, 208, 256, 262–63; IV, 293, 296, 325, 352, 353; V, 367, 441, 447; VI, 477, 483, 526, 532, 533; VII, 566, 588, 596, 597, 622; VIII, 669, 670, 686, 687, 710; IX, 734, 746, 747, 796, 800, 801, 806; X, 828, 854; XI, 934, 935; XII, 1018, 1019, 1026
  burning of, II, 139, 145, 151, 172
White Plains, Battle of, I, 16; II, 161
Whitman, Walt, IV, 307; VII, 557
Wickersham, George W., VIII, 703
Wilderness, Battle of the (1775), I, 29
Wilderness, Battle of the (1864), V, 418
William and Mary, College of, I, 49; II, 96, 97, 113, 134
Williamsburg, Va., II, 96, 134; 160
Willkie, Wendell L., X, 857–58, 861, 882, 883
Wilmot Proviso, IV, 312, 338
Wilson, Charles E., XI, 954–55, 956, 972, 973
Wilson, Edith Bolling Galt, IX, 734–35, 736, 737, 740, 741, 742, 754, 763
Wilson, Eleanor Randolph, IX, 734, 746, 747
Wilson, Ellen Louise Axson, IX, 726, 734, 746
Wilson, Henry, VI, 490, 508
Wilson, James, I, 48; II, 142
Wilson, Jessie Woodrow, IX, 734, 746, 747

ACKNOWLEDGMENTS

The Editors are grateful to these individuals and organizations for their invaluable assistance in the picture research for this project:

Adams National Historic Site: Wilhelmina Harris
Charles Baptie
Bowdoin College: Joseph D. Kamin
Buffalo & Erie County Historical Society: Paul F. Redding
Chicago Historical Society: Mary Frances Rhymer
Cincinnati Historical Society: Lee Jordan; Eleanor Wirmel
Colonial Williamsburg: Hugh DeSamper; Marguerite Gignilliat
John Coolidge
J. Doyle DeWitt
Eastman House: Beaumont Newhall
General Dwight D. Eisenhower
Grouseland: Mrs. Charles A. Hamke
The Hermitage: Stephen S. Lawrence
Harding Memorial Association: Warren C. Sawyer
Benjamin Harrison Home: Ruth Woodworth
Rutherford B. Hayes Library: Watt P. Marchman
Independence Hall: James R. Sullivan
Indiana Historical Society: Caroline Dunn
Andrew Johnson Home: Margaret Johnson Patterson Bartlett
Lyndon B. Johnson
Mrs. Joseph P. Kennedy
Stanley King
Paulus Leeser
Library of Congress: Virginia Daiker; Renata Shaw
Sidney Mayer

Metropolitan Museum of Art: Margaret Nolan
Mount Vernon: Christine Meadows
James Monroe Memorial Library: Laurence Gouverneur Hoes
National Gallery of Art: Ruth Dundas
National Archives: Josephine Cobb
National Broadcasting Company: Dan Jones
National Portrait Gallery: Robert G. Stewart
New-York Historical Society: Carolyn Scoon; Wilson G. Duprey
New York Public Library: Romana Javitz
Ohio Historical Society: Elizabeth R. Martin
James K. Polk Home: Sibyl A. Whelchel
Presidential Libraries: Herman Kahn
Franklin D. Roosevelt Library: Elizabeth B. Drewry; Joseph Marshall; William Stickle
Theodore Roosevelt Association: Helen MacLachlan
Richard Rudisill
Sagamore Hill National Historic Site: Mrs. Harold Kraft
Smithsonian Institution: Meredith Johnson
Tennessee State Library & Archives: Harriet C. Owsley
Time-Life, Inc.: Valerie Vondermuhl
Harry S. Truman Library: Philip C. Brooks; Cecil Smith
United States Defense Department: Colonel Robert A. Webb
United States Military Academy: J. Thomas Russell; Kenneth W. Rapp
United States Supreme Court: T. Perry Lippitt
Virginia State Library: Katherine M. Smith
Wheatland: Claire Parker
The White House: James R. Ketchum
Woodrow Wilson Home: Ruth L. Dillon

WELCOME THE PRESIDENT
SOODO WOMEN'S TEACHERS COLLEGE ATTACHED
RESIDENT & MRS. JOHNSON
COLLEGE